GERANIUM GROWING

BY
H. G. WITHAM FOGG

W. & G. FOYLE LTD
119-125, CHARING CROSS ROAD, W.C.2

First published 1955
Reprinted May 1957

Printed in Great Britain by
BILLING & SONS LTD.
GUILDFORD AND LONDON
H4267

CONTENTS

INTRODUCTION

IT seems that although the Geranium is such a widely grown plant there are so few books devoted to its history and cultivation. This always appears to have been the case, for although it is true that during the Victorian era the Geranium was *the* plant to grow, for both outdoor summer bedding and greenhouse and conservatory decoration, there never seems to have been much simple, yet comprehensive literature on the subject.

There were certainly a number of short pamphlets, but these were either very brief and incomplete or in some other language, and none of these now seem to be available.

There were two standard works on the Geranium, which because of common usage, is the term generally applied to the plants, which are strictly speaking, Pelargoniums, but these have long since gone out of print. The first, *A Monograph of the Genus Geranium*, was published in London in 1805. A handsome volume of quarto size, its price to-day is around £300 and it is therefore a collectors' book, rather than one within the reach of the average gardener. The second is the better known and more frequently referred to, *Geraniaceæ*, by R. Sweet, first published in London in 1820. It is in five volumes and additionally valuable because of its 500 coloured illustrations. This, too, is out of print and very expensive, and to be found only in libraries not usually accessible to the general public. There was, however, published in New York in 1946 a book by Helen van Pelt Wilson with the title *Geraniums, Pelargoniums for Windows and Gardens*. This is really intended for American gardeners, although, naturally, it contains some good general information.

In 1951 Mr. J. E. Cross, one of the founders of the Geranium Society, published his volume *The Book of the Geranium*, a first-class publication which meets a real need. There is no doubt that the cult of the Geranium is fast returning, and this present handbook is written in response to a definite and constant demand for a simple treatise.

The intention in writing it is to bring within the reach of the ordinary gardener a handbook which will, without being

involved or difficult to understand, contain just the information
needed regarding the general culture and upkeep, whether a
large bed, window box, hanging basket, vase or flower-pot is
being planted with Geraniums. In addition, it seeks to give
some interesting details which it is hoped will increase the love
of the Geranium in its widest sense. Even with such a good-
tempered plant to deal with, there are always problems which
arise concerning such things as the best varieties to grow, right
soil, propagation and training, and the dealing with pests and
diseases should these ever occur. It is the object of this book
to give information built on just such things as these. Care
has been taken to avoid the use of technical terms and to keep
to everyday language, which will enable all who grow Geraniums, however inexperienced they may be, to gain pleasure
and satisfaction from such an interesting hobby. In addition,
it is hoped that the more experienced grower and raiser of
plants for sale, will at least find the pages of this little book to
be entertaining.

I would like to express my gratitude to the Botanical Society
of South Africa for their permission to use information, from
an article by Mrs. F. M. Leighton, on the early history of the
Pelargonium which appears on page 7.

I am also grateful to Mrs. Romanne-James for the legend of
the Geranium, whilst a special word of thanks is due to Mr. H.
Champneys, editor of *The Garden*, for his help in providing
some of the photographs.

1

PAST AND PRESENT

THE name Geranium or Crane's Bill has its origin in antiquity, having been used by both Dioscorides and Pliny. As recorded by F. M. Leighton in the *Journal of the Botanical Society of South Africa*, the name as defined by Linnæus in his *Species Plantarum* of 1753 comprised three distinct genera, viz. Geranium proper or Crane's Bill, Pelargonium or Stork's Bill and Erodium or Heron's Bill. These names are descriptive of the shape of the fruit. The genera Pelargonium and Erodium were created by a French botanist, L'Héritier, in 1788. The true Geranium is a cosmopolitan genus, of which about eight species are native to South Africa. It is seldom cultivated as an ornamental garden plant in South Africa, although a number of introduced species and a few species of Erodium as well, occur as weeds.

Pelargoniums are distinguished from Geraniums by their irregular flowers, the nectariferous spur which adheres to the pedicel, and by the shape of the fruit.

Pelargonium, though largely South African in origin, extends to Madagascar and up to the east coast of Africa, to Arabia and western India. There are species in Australia and on Tristan da Cunha. From the South African species have arisen all the manifold varieties of Pelargonium and so-called "Ivy-leafed and Zonal Geraniums" of horticulture.

Some botanical writers of the early nineteenth century insisted on following the usage of Linnæus and declined to accept the new name Pelargonium. Among these was H. C. Andrews, whose prolific writing and whose popularity among gardeners of his day, have probably had much to do with the persistence of the name Geranium for a large section of the garden varieties of Pelargonium. In the preface to his monumental work on Geranium, published about 1820, Andrews says: "If such generic divisions, that is the splitting of Linnæus's genus into Geranium, Erodium and Pelargonium, were generally adopted, the approach to botanic science would be so choked up with ill-shaped, useless lumber that, like a castle in a fairy tale guarded by hideous dwarfs, none but a Botanic Quixote would

attempt investigation." The genus Pelargonium is accepted
by botanists to-day—quixotic or otherwise.

Among the hardy plants which were collected by early visitors
to the Cape, and which survived the voyage to Europe, was
Pelargonium Triste, a humble plant of the sandy flats and lower
slopes. It is a low-growing, rather inconspicuous plant, which
attracts little attention from modern gardeners.

Thomas Johnson, in his edition of Gerard's *Herball* published in 1633, refers to it as follows: "There is of late brought
into his kingdome, and to our knowledge by the industry of
Mr John Tradescant, another more rare and no less beautifull
than any of the former, hee had it by the name of Geranium
indicum noctu ordoratum; this hath not as yet been written
of by any that I know; therefore I will give you the description
thereof, but cannot as yet give you the figure, because I omitted
the taking thereof the last yeare, and it has not as yet come to
his perfection. The leaves are larger, being almost a foot long,
composed of sundry little leaves of an unequal bigness, set upon
a thick and stiff middle rib, and these leaves are much divided
and cut in . . . they are thicke, green and somewhat hairie:
the stalke is thicke and some cubit high; at the top of each
branch, upon foot stalkes some inch long, grows some eleven
or twelve floures, and each of the floures consisteth of five round
pointed leaves of a yellowish colour, with a large blacke-purple
spot in the middle of each leafe, as it were painted, which
gives the floure a great deal of beauty; and it also hath a good
smell. I did see it in floure about the end of July 1632 being
the first time that it floured with the owner thereof. We may
fitly call it Sweet Indian Storks bill or painted Storksbill; and
in Latin, Geranium Indicum odoratum, flore maculato."

The inclusion of the word *Indicum* shows that, as with a
number of other Cape plants taken to Europe by ships returning from the East, *Pelargonium Triste* was thought to have
come from India or the Indies. John Tradescant's garden was
in Lambeth, South London.

In 1635 Parkinson wrote of *P. Triste*: "The flowers smell
very sweete, like Muske in the night onely, and not at all in
the day time, as refusing the Sunnes influence but delighteth
in the Moones appearance."

The next reference to this species is in 1668 in Florens
Schuyl's Catalogue of the Leyden Botanic Gardens. It is listed
among the introductions from the Cape of Good Hope. When

Paul Hermann published his catalogue of these gardens in 1687 the number of "geraniums" from the Cape had risen to ten. Hermann had visited the Cape about 1672 and tells us that he found *P. Cucullatum* growing at the foot of Table Mountain.

From Aiton's catalogue of the plants cultivated at the Royal Botanic Gardens, Kew, published in 1759, we learn that it was introduced in 1690 by Mr. Bentick.

With the advent of the more spectacular and colourful Pelargoniums, *P. Triste* seems to have fallen from favour, although it was still grown in European gardens. A coloured picture appeared in Curtis's *Botanical Magazine* in 1814.

During the eighteenth century many of our Pelargoniums found their way into European gardens. Among these was *P. Inquinans*, one of the progenitors of the many types of red "Geranium". It first made its appearance in literature in the *Hortus Elthamensis* of Dillenius in 1732, and Aiton says that it was cultivated as early as 1714 by Bishop Compton, a bishop of London, who seems to have shown a marked interest in botany in general and in South African plants in particular. He acquired, when on a visit to Holland, a codex which probably included some of the Claudius drawings from the Cape (or copies of them).

The forerunner of the "Ivy-leafed Geranium", *P. Peltatum*, was introduced into Holland in 1700 by Willem Adriaan van der Stel. The seeds came from the "region of Heycoon". Seeds of *P. Zonale* were sent in the same year from the "region of the Attaqua".

With these, and others, established in gardens during the seventeenth and eighteenth centuries, hybrids began to arise.

Although the names Geranium and Pelargonium are well known to most gardeners, it is not always realised quite what they are or their difference. Both belong to the natural order Geraniaceæ and the confusion in the use of the two names is not altogether surprising. The true Geranium is to be found in several of our native species long admired as wild flowers, of which the Herb Robert, *Geranium Robertianum,* with its pretty pink flowers, so frequently seen growing alongside country lanes and roads. There are a number of other wildlings, but for the most part they are not worthy of much consideration. The cultivated section of the Hardy Geraniums will be dealt with later.

The word Pelargonium comes from *pelargos*, which literally

means a stork, in allusion to the beak-like form of the seed pod. Similarity in the derivation of the names Geranium and Pelargonium—Crane's Bill and Stork's Bill—is sufficient to indicate the reason for the confusion and ambiguity which often occurs in the use of the names. Furthermore, another part of the Geraniaceæ, the Erodiums, which are also referred to later, are commonly known as Heron's Bill.

However, there are botanical differences between the Geranium and Pelargonium, and, simply put, we may say that whereas the petals of the former are regular in shape without spurs and have ten stamens, the Pelargonium has irregular petals, often only two or three upper ones, the remainder being very small, the flowers being spurred with not more than five stamens.

The well-known bedding Geraniums, so often seen in many brilliant coloured varieties, of which Paul Crampel has long been the best known, is, strictly speaking, *Pelargonium Zonale*. The original species itself had and has, in its native habitat of South Africa, foliage with a dark horseshoe zone, which accounts for the designation Zonale.

Many of the modern varieties of the species have entirely unmarked leaves, without even a trace of the darker zoning, although they are true Pelargonium Zonal hybrids. Here it might be said that the tremendous number of Zonal Pelargoniums now in cultivation have come, not entirely from Zonale itself, but from that species and *P. Inquinans*. It would appear evident that much of the bolder type of flower, as well as the size of the truss and the rather succulent appearance of the foliage, is due to the influence of *P. Inquinans*. It is also probable that the absence of the zonal or horseshoe markings in many varieties is due to the same parent.

The Show or Regal Pelargonium is *P. Domesticum*, which has been grown in Britain for very many years, while in America they are known as Martha Washingtons. These have very large blooms in many striking colours and are really best when grown under glass. Few, if any, of the Regals will flower during the winter, which the Zonals frequently do, but they are an admirable subject for giving a showy display from the early summer onwards, when they frequently appear as pot plants in the house and never fail to attract attention when exhibited at flower shows. In addition, in sheltered gardens they may be used out of doors with great advantage, if given

SHOWING FOLIAGE AND TUBEROUS ROOTS OF
Pelargonium triste

the background of a low wall or fence. As cut flowers, too, they are occasionally used for bouquets and decorative purposes, when the beautifully marked and blotched flowers give a charming, exotic display without appearing gaudy or flamboyant. It will be easily realised why Regal and Show varieties were so popular a century ago, for their richly coloured blooms of substance have that comfortable peaceful look, characteristic of that time. Geraniums have always held an attraction for me, the reason for which it is not easy to determine. Certainly it is not that I like very formal beds, with scarlet Geraniums massed or dotted about like soldiers standing stiffly to attention.

One of my earliest memories on entering into nursery training is the sight of a rather stern, yet really kindly, foreman sitting hours on end at the propagating bench, carefully, but with great ease, taking cuttings of many varieties of Geraniums, some of which are now most difficult to obtain. Hour by hour he would sit, scarcely saying a word, but just continuing to take his cuttings, of which many came from material brought back to the nursery when gardens, which were regularly maintained, were being cleared of summer bedding plants in readiness for putting in the spring-flowering bulbs. I remember, too, the thousands of pots of rooted cuttings which had to be kept free from discoloured leaves and bracts, and which regularly each week, had to be moved along the greenhouse bench so that they did not stand in one place too long!

Also vivid in my memory, are many visits made to Covent Garden market in the early mornings and the sight of trays and boxes of Geraniums in many varieties and of hearing salesmen and buyers discussing Crampels, Denmarks, Crousses, Galilees and Rivals which were, and still are, greatly in demand, since they are all entirely reliable varieties.

Perhaps at the bottom of all my liking for Geraniums is the name, which comes from the old Greek word *Geranos*, literally meaning a crane and so given because of the likeness of the seed vessels to the head and beak of that bird. This shapeliness is not accidental, but, as we shall presently see, it is one of Nature's ways of ensuring that the seed, when self-sown, really finds its way into the soil, so as to be able to germinate and not be left lying on the surface to dry out and decay.

The natural order Geraniaceæ takes in numerous families and species of plants, but we are not here concerned with plants such as Impatiens and Oxalis, which are included in the order, since we are considering only Geraniums, as they are best known, which takes in the hardy sorts, Erodiums, Regal Pelargoniums, and the well-known Zonal and Ivy-leaved varieties.

There are probably many more gardeners in Britain to-day than there were, but there was definitely a quality about many of the gardeners and gardens of a century ago which gave them something of a romantic air. Certainly it was not only the old type of formal garden or the elaborate landscape creations which were once so much in favour, which made the Victorian gardeners and their cultures stand out.

It was, I think, a great affection for what we are inclined to call the simpler, old-fashioned flowers, which gave them a value which continues to remain, even although we no longer like the older methods of layout. For in spite of the massive delphiniums, lupins, phlox and gladioli, there is something about those old favourites such as sweet william, ranunculuses, auriculas, primulas, polyanthuses and stocks which continues to appeal.

These are the subjects which for many years, in fact centuries, have kept alive and transmitted an interest in the growing of the less spectacular, but nevertheless intrinsically beautiful, flowers. There is a record of a colony of Flemish weavers holding a florists' feast in Norwich in the year 1637, when it was the flowers just mentioned which received great attention and provided great fascination, not only to local people, but to those of many other towns. One of the results was that a friendly rivalry was created, and this in turn led to the formation of flower shows in various parts of the country. A peculiar thing about this increase of flower growing, was that certain towns seemed to favour and grow almost exclusively, a particular type of plant. Since many of the ordinary people became interested in flowers and their culture, it was no longer only the gentry or monied classes who were concerned, but it was, so it seemed, an indication of the skill and ingenuity of weavers and operatives that they were able to carry over to the raising and cultivation of the flower of their choice, something of their ability to create new colours and shapes. It was a criterion of success when a precise pattern or colour was obtained, and it was the clear, brilliant hues which were sought and not the multicoloured shot effects so often seen to-day.

In all this change, which meant that the ordinary man and woman could now grow flowers as well as the rich, the Geranium which had come from Cape Colony, South Africa, soon earned for itself a place of affection, and because of its ease of culture, plants were soon seen in almost every cottage window. This did much to brighten the dingy homes of the working classes, but at the same time it was also considered to be a plant for the aristocrat and was to be found in the conservatories and hothouses of the largest establishments. In the early part of the nineteenth century—1805 to be exact—there was published in London a *Monograph of the Genus Geranium*, and in 1820 R. Sweet published his *Geraniaceæ*, a comprehensive work in five volumes, which is still regarded as a standard guide of the earlier Pelargonium species and hybrids, many of which are now unobtainable. Even so, the hand-coloured illustrations of these species make the book extremely valuable, in

spite of the fact that it does not contain the better-known
Zonal Geraniums of the present time.

These publications certainly kindled a greater interest in the
Geranium family, which one might almost say achieved its
greatest popularity just at the time of Queen Victoria's acces-
sion to the throne and remained in vogue during the whole of
her long reign, increasing in the high esteem of the public
during each year of Victoria's rule. During that period no
garden was complete without this easy-to-grow flower, and
every conservatory was ablaze with the showy blooms in many
colours, for Geraniums are not all scarlet but take in many
attractive shades.

With the passing of the Queen came a distinct change in the
attitude of both the gardener and general public. Like many
other things so characteristic of that peaceful era, the Geranium
became neglected and despised. Perhaps this was only in line
with the turning from the formal gardens to a more easy and
less exacting method of planting, with fewer straight lines,
squares, oblongs, diamonds and ribbons, which, of course, all
tended to give a very stiff and rather forbidding appearance.

Whilst it may have no significance at all, it does seem remarkable that with the passing of the old-fashioned method of bedding out, in which Geraniums played so large a part, there also
passed to a very great extent, the chivalry and gentleness of the
Victorian period. Although this is not the place to enter into
such matters, it does seem evident that there also vanished a
great deal of the concern for the well-being of one for another,
a lesser desire for public worship and the recognition of
spiritual values, with a greater inclination "to get and to hold".

What is significant, is the fact that after two terrible world
wars there has come a real and definite return to favour of the
Geranium. This may be but a coincidence, but I think that it
is a faint indication that the Geranium, so inseparably connected with those calm Victorian times, is but a reminder of
those happier days before such things as rockets or hydrogen
bombs were ever conceived. Conversely, since there is now a
definite return to favour of this most adaptable plant, and the
Geranium Society formed in 1952 is a sure indication of a much
greater interest and demand, one can sincerely hope that, in
spite of the unrest and continued occurrence of international
crises, the restful and placid appearance of the Geranium may
be a sign that calmer times are in store for the world.

A point of great interest to me, has been to see that more and more Geraniums, including the variegated-leaved varieties, are being used in parks and public gardens, as well as in the laying-out of summer beds in prominent roadside positions. In addition to the ornamental foliaged sorts, the lively colours available, serve to set off to advantage some of the rather severe-looking modern buildings, near which they are often planted.

Another advantage in growing the Zonal Geranium is that an individual plant will last for many years and it may be almost continuously propagated by taking cuttings, although perhaps the two most suitable times for this operation are in the spring and the early autumn. They will certainly repay all the care and attention bestowed upon them, and it is doubtful if there is any other so easily grown plant, which has flowers with such intensity and purity of colour.

Let it be understood, too, that although the Regal varieties are the more generally thought of as the greenhouse section, the Zonals are also first class for this purpose; in fact, whereas the former are for the most part spring and summer flowering, the Zonals can by proper treatment, be had in bloom without undue trouble throughout the whole of the winter.

Very many flower growers will be familiar with the book *Down Your Garden Path* by Beverley Nichols, who writes in such an interesting way about his garden and what befell him in the making of it. Amid the humour there is much that is of a practical value to the gardener.

TYPICAL STORK'S BILL-SHAPED SEED PODS

In another novel, *Laughter on the Stairs*, the same author writes, as only he can, in an amusing way concerning Geraniums. He says: "Geraniums to me are a sort of test flower, for long experience has told me that people who do not like Geraniums have something morally unsound about them. Sooner or later you will find them out, you will discover that they drink or steal or speak sharply to cats. Never trust a man or woman who is not passionately devoted to Geraniums."

The Pelargonium is very free in producing new forms, and this is one of the reasons for the confusion which has arisen in regard to naming and classification. In addition, different names are used in other countries for the same variety. For instance, in the United States, Skelly's Pride is known as Jean, and many other Zonals and Regals have entirely different titles.

However, both the British and American Geranium Societies are fully aware of the muddle that there is in nomenclature, and they are taking steps to establish an authoritative system of registration. It is planned to have a system, as with other plants, whereby proposed names for new introductions are first submitted for approval, instead of anyone giving a name to any plant of their choice, however similar it may be to a variety already in commerce.

The following is a condensed résumé of suggestions proposed and likely to be accepted by the International Geranium and Pelargonium Society, and no doubt the Geranium Society of this country will agree to these or very similar proposals.

1. The term "variety" (abbreviated var. or v.) is reserved for those forms which are known to occur in the wild and which have names in Latin.

2. The term *"cultivar"* (abbreviated cv.) is applied to those special forms which have originated or are maintained only in cultivation.

3. The name and descriptions must be published in a dated catalogue, technical work or periodical. (Plants registered by the Society will be published in the Society magazine.)

4. No cultivar names should be in Latin.

5. A cultivar name should be used only once in the same genus.

6. A cultivar name should consist of not more than two words.

7. When naming cultivars after persons, avoid such forms as

"Mr.", "Mrs.", "Sir" or first-name initials: thus "Ellen Will-mott" is acceptable, but not "Mrs. Ellen Willmott", "E. Will-mott", "Mrs. Willmott" or "Mrs. E. Willmott".

8. The articles "A" and "The", unless required by linguistic custom, should be avoided: thus "La Rochelle" is acceptable but not "The Colonel".

9. Abbreviations for personal and geographical names should be avoided: thus "William Thomas" and "Mount Kisco" are acceptable, but not "Wm. Thomas" and "Mt. Kisco".

Registration will not be restricted to new introductions. In fact, the success of the programme depends in large measure on the registration of established cultivars. The applicant will be required to provide a specimen of the subject plant. These specimens will be used in assembling an authentic collection of registered plants to provide a direct method of identification and comparison.

2

THE USES OF THE GERANIUM

JUST as there is a legend about rosemary and the way its flowers turned blue after Mary the Mother of Christ hung her robes to dry on a rosemary bush, so there is an Eastern legend concerning the Geranium. It is one of Moslem origin and connected with the marsh mallow.

This particular mallow was, so the tale runs, the only plant of its kind. One day the prophet Mohamet was taking his customary walk when he found himself in unfrequented country. It was very hot. The sun was shining fiercely on his body. To obtain relief he took off his shirt and rinsed it in a nearby pool, around which grew a quantity of marsh mallow plants. After the rinsing, Mohamet hung the garment on to the branches of an overhanging tree to dry. As it hung there, water from the shirt dripped down on to one of the mallows, which immediately turned into a most beautiful Geranium plant, while the other mallows growing around the pool retained their original appearance.

Many years ago the leaves of the ordinary red Geranium, which were in cultivation well before the origin of Paul

Crampel, were used as a healing agent in cases of wounds made by any kind of iron or metal. There is evidently some great healing property in these leaves, for whether the actual leaves themselves were applied to the wounds, first being lightly moistened to make them adhere to the flesh, or made into an infusion and the resultant liquid dabbed into the wound, healing soon began, even in the case of most difficult instances.

The wild *Geranium Robertianum*, or Herb Robert, and *G. Pratense* have also been much used in medicine, although not in recent years. It is evident, however, that they were greatly relied upon long ago for several important purposes, including the arresting of internal bleeding, as an astringent in connection with kidney troubles and also as a tonic. The sweet-scented Rose Geranium—it is the leaves which are scented—is a native of the Cape of Good Hope, and the French are believed to have been the first to discover that an oil—Geraniol—could be extracted from the foliage; in fact, this French oil is still said to be the finest of its kind on the market.

Pelargonium Capitatum, the proper name of this species, has what can be described as a strong, rather acid rose scent, and apart from the oil or essence referred to, a preserve is made from the leaves. This is of a clear green colour and is known as Geranium Jelly. In the South of France and parts of Algeria, *P. Capitatum* is cultivated by the acre for these commercial purposes. In warm climates the Rose Geranium is grown as a shrubby plant and usually reaches four feet in height. In this country it is necessary to grow it permanently under glass, although the plants do well where they are placed out of doors during the summer, when they usually develop into strong, sturdy bushes.

They are then lifted in September and put in large tubs or pots, according to the size of the plants, and kept under glass and out of the frost during the winter. The leaves of the Rose Geranium are covered with soft hairs and the scent is both spicy and rose-like. They are sometimes used in cooking and especially to impart a rose-like flavour to custard puddings and jellies, which, thus flavoured, were once considered great delicacies, suitable for producing on the most important occasions.

The leaves of this same variety can be employed to make a pretty garnish for sweet dishes, and so used, nearly always cause attention, surprise and pleasure.

Rose Geraniums have a further valuable use in perfuming

castor sugar for sprinkling on cakes and other confectionery. The method is to put a few leaves into a stoppered jar of castor sugar. Leave them there for a few days, when their presence will thoroughly permeate the sugar so that when it is used it will have a very pleasing taste and, in addition, as was once much more widely believed and acted upon, the Geranium flavour will produce relief from various stomach discomforts. Rose Geranium and other scented-leaved species were once gathered, bruised and put in jars in which there was a little slightly warmed water, and used, after standing for some time in a corked bottle, for dabbing on the arms and neck "before leaving the house". At one time, too, it was claimed that an extract from Geraniums had great power in the healing of gout, hernia and other internal disorders.

In addition, at one time no bouquet or basket of flowers was considered complete unless it contained several varieties of scented Geraniums. The leaves were also greatly in favour in making up potpourris. There are many recipes for this, and although they may vary considerably in detail, there is one underlying principle in the make-up of all of them, and that is the ingredients used must be added in such proportions so that the scent of one cannot kill the perfumes of the others. In this connection the scented-leaved Geraniums have the quality of blending with almost any other scented leaves and flowers, and yet retain their own scent, without impairing the smell of the remaining items.

Potpourri is made up either dry or moist, the former being the easiest and quickest. Although rose petals, violet, jasmine and lavender flowers, verbena, sweet herbs and bay leaves should be the base of the mixture, it is the scented Geranium leaves along with a spice mixture which provide the essential and long-lasting scent. The flowers and leaves must first be dried, and a simple way of doing this is to spread them out on sheets of paper in an airy room, preferably in the semi-dark, or they can be placed on flat trays in a not too warm airing cupboard.

The material used in little silk bags or ornamental envelopes, known as sachet powders, also had the scented Geraniums in a good proportion of their make-up, while when it was fashionable to use snuff, several kinds were rendered aromatic by the use of perfumes containing roses, bergamot or Geraniums.

It is certain that three or four centuries ago the use of perfumes was very popular, even among the most ordinary folk,
and in many old books can be found recipes for many kinds of
flower conserves, perfumed powders and ointments, wash-balls
and sweet bags and fragrant cushions. The latter were much
used until comparatively recent times, being hung on the backs
and wings of armchairs, where they proved a source of interest
to the visitor who leaned back in the chair, this action causing
a fresh stirring of the perfume.

Perhaps the so-called sweet bags are the most interesting of
all the very old uses for scents in which the Geranium was
largely employed. There are various recorded recipes for
these, and reference too can be found in old literature on
"bags to smell into, for melancholy or to cause one to sleep".
One of these recommendations was dried rose leaves, scented
Geranium leaves, powdered mint and cloves, which if "put
together in a bag and taken to bed with you, will cause sleep,
besides being good to smell at other times".

As previously indicated, it has been the custom for many
years to use Geranium leaves for the flavouring of jellies and
custards, and both gooseberry and apple jellies assume a really
lively taste when flavoured in this way. It has also been the
custom of country women for many years to use Geranium
leaves as a flavouring for cakes, and of recent date there have
been many references to "Geranium cakes". The method is to
lay six to eight leaves of the scented Oak-leaved Geranium at
the bottom of the cake tin before the mixture, either ordinary
sponge or Victoria sponge, is poured in. When cooked the
leaves can be removed, and the delicate flavour is imparted to
the whole cake.

3

GENERAL CULTURAL REQUIREMENTS

SINCE there are no two growers who have the exact conditions
for growing Pelargoniums, it is impossible to give precise
details for culture, for so much does depend on individual
circumstances. The plants have, however, certain requirements which are needed for real success, whether few or many

plants are being grown by either the raw amateur or the experienced professional grower.

It has long been said that Geraniums grow best in poor soil, otherwise they will produce all foliage and no flowers. Again, it has frequently been asserted that the plants should be kept dry at the roots. Neither of these statements is correct; in fact, although the plants *will* grow in impoverished soil, to do really well, they must have a rooting medium in which there is plenty of goodness. It will just not do to use any old garden soil for growing plants in pots. For potting up at any time of the year, the John Innes potting composts are invaluable. These are standardised and generally available in three grades and require next to no extras mixed with them, since they are so composed as to provide sufficient nourishment until the plants are potted up into large receptacles. The make-up of this compost is as follows: John Innes Potting Compost No. 1, seven parts clean fibrous loam, three parts peat, two parts coarse silver sand, and to each bushel of the mixture is added three-quarters of an ounce of chalk and a quarter pound of base fertiliser, which consists of two parts hoof and horn meal, two parts superphosphate and one of potash, all by weight. The John Innes Potting Compost No. 2 has a double portion of base fertiliser and the No. 3 treble proportion.

These composts have proved to be quite sufficient to produce good plants, although if it is decided to add additional fertiliser as growth proceeds, avoid using those which are likely to cause rapid growth, which really means those which have an analysis showing a high percentage of nitrogen.

Perhaps one may wonder why ordinary garden soil is not recommended for potting purposes. It can be used, of course, but a good potting mixture—not fancy mixtures containing artificials of unknown quantity or quality which so often lead to forced growth and the breakdown of the plant tissues—contains organic matter which holds moisture better than garden soil. These good composts are so made up as to be open and porous, promoting proper aeration and drainage. Although the John Innes composts are good, they do contain inorganic compounds, and for that reason it must not be assumed that they are indispensable, for an ideal mixture can be made up with sweet loam, peat or leaf mould, silver sand and bone meal, and decayed sifted manure.

The modern theory that diseases must be expected is unsound, and I thoroughly believe that the frequency of their appearance nowadays in almost any plant one cares to mention, is in the majority of cases, due to wrong feeding and the use of so many chemicals and chemico-biological treatments, applied on the flimsiest of pretexts, and to a very large extent by mal-nutrition or partial starvation, which has its beginning in wrong feeding. It is also a mistaken idea that to cure disease, some kind of poisonous spray must be applied. Poison can never bring good health; the real answer to disease being healthy stock, hygienic conditions and proper nourishment.

Having made sure that the right soil for a good rooting medium is provided, the plants have several small but important requirements if real success is to be achieved. Fortunately these do not include the provision of a large greenhouse or any expensive-to-run routine to ensure success. In fact, the plants thrive in the smallest type of glass structure, provided that in addition to their proper soil requirements being met, they have light, ventilation, the right temperature and moisture as required, and we will consider them in that order.

It is elementary to say that without light the leaves of the plants become yellow, which is an indication of the absence of chlorophyll, the substance of the green cells of the leaves; for nearly everyone has seen plants which have been kept in the dark for some time, with the result that the leaves have yellowed and eventually become colourless. This is particularly so when there is heat as well, since then, not only does growth become soft and pale, but the whole plant is weakened with few, if any, flowers being produced.

With the many types of greenhouses now available the accent has been to ensure all possible light reaching the plants being grown, and many houses have sides entirely of glass. On the other hand, it is sometimes necessary to give some kind of shading during mid-summer. Not a lot is needed; in fact, just sufficient to prevent the rays of the sun from falling directly on to the plants. The Pelargonium, being of South African origin, likes sun of course, but glass is inclined to bring about leaf scorch and other troubles as well as drying out the compost quickly and causing the blooms to become bleached. Where blinds are fitted to the house they are ideal for shading, since they can be used as required. Strips of hessian or even paper can be fixed up just to keep off the direct rays of the sun.

Failing this, whiting or Summer Cloud can be painted on to
the glass, although with these there is the bother of washing
them off later.

The question of temperature is an important one as far as
the Pelargonium is concerned, and equally important is ventilation, for by this means it is possible to ensure that the plants
do not become weak and drawn and therefore susceptible to
disease.

Most glasshouses are well fitted with ventilators but, even so,
common sense is necessary in their use, for when opened, they
not only let out the hot air but also admit more fresh air, so
that they must be used in such a way as to avoid draughts,
being opened before the heat becomes very great and closed to
prevent very low night temperatures. Regularity in giving
ventilation is a necessity. As far as possible, a temperature
around sixty degrees Fahrenheit should be considered the
ideal, although in summer it will probably rise at periods to
considerably more. This is the time that proper ventilation is
essential. During the coldest months it may not be possible to
raise the temperature more than fifty degrees with an even
lower drop at night, but definite steps should be made to ensure
that it does not fall below forty-five degrees, particularly if one
is aiming at having winter or very early spring flowers.

Experience has proved that although Pelargoniums will stand
fluctuations in temperature, they will not do well in continuous
great heat. For keeping the plants in healthy condition with
foliage of good colour, a very dry atmosphere should be avoided,
so that in general an occasional damping of the greenhouse
floor and staging should be given, to provide the humid conditions necessary for good results.

What about moisture requirements? This is a question which
demands attention, for even if soil make-up, temperature and
ventilation are right, if the plant's roots are kept either too dry
or too wet, trouble is bound to occur. Pelargoniums will certainly stand hard treatment but they will not survive without
moisture, which is being absorbed by the roots all the time.
Having provided good drainage for the receptacles in which the
plants are growing, it is only natural that the water applied
will be used fairly quickly and will need regular replacement.
Even in winter a little moisture will be required at times by
established plants, for the belief that no water is needed by
Pelargoniums during the shortest days is a fallacy.

Pelargoniums are not hardy and frost will destroy them, although so long as the foliage and stem are dry, they will stand low temperatures fairly well, but if moisture is present or the roots are in soggy soil the plants will soon be injured. This is one reason why the plants require so little watering during the winter.

In avoiding damp conditions during the winter, care must be taken not to go to the other extreme, and the practice as is sometimes advised, of knocking the plants out of pots and tying the roots in bundles and then hanging them up in the greenhouse or shed during the winter, is nothing short of folly. The fact that occasionally some plants have survived despite this bad treatment is a further indication of how good tempered the plant is.

As to the means of heating the greenhouse or other glass structure being used, there are several good ways of doing this, and although hot-water pipes still provide the ideal method of giving the warmth needed, there are now many electric heaters which are easy to work and regulate and not expensive to use. Of these there are some which can be thermostatically controlled, and once set the thermostat maintains the required temperature. Gas heating, too, is sometimes employed, but in this connection it is essential that no fumes enter the house, otherwise the plants are bound to suffer. Where no other method is practicable, oil lamps can be used, and while not ideal there are many instances of complete success being achieved by this means, although here again no fumes should be allowed to escape among the plants. This is often a difficulty, but provided the oil stove is kept clean, regularly trimmed and not handled carelessly so as to spill the oil, such stoves can be quite efficient. In this connection, the Eltex oil-burning greenhouse heater can be recommended with confidence. It is rigidly constructed in galvanised sheet steel, has easily removable lamps which can be filled without difficulty, and a detachable moisture tray which helps to provide an atmosphere which does not become too dry or fume laden.

Both when fresh plants are brought in and when moving plants into larger pots, a little soil should be scraped from the top of the ball of earth, so as to get rid of any fine moss or green algæ which so often develops with pot-grown plants, and as it is such an important point it is again stressed that Geraniums in pots do better if the pots are on the small side, for then growth will be somewhat restricted and the flowers are more freely produced if the plants are rather pot-bound.

If the soil is nicely moist the potting operation will be a simple job with little root destruction. See that the plants are placed just a little deeper than they were previously grown, but make sure that no leaf stalks are buried, for to do so would be to encourage decay and disease. It is best to pot hard, for it is the plants with firm stems which are more likely to be the most floriferous.

Geraniums do not usually wilt as do other plants when their roots are dry, but nevertheless serious damage is liable to occur if moisture is withheld, the evidence being that the foliage yellows and falls off prematurely.

Many fancy receptacles are available nowadays, but the long-used ordinary flower-pots are very suitable, since they are porous, which helps to keep the soil in the pots from becoming too wet and sour. Even when plants are repotted from time to time there are occasions when food will be needed, and while it is possible to apply a good general fertiliser, the accent should definitely be on one of an organic nature, and the use of liquid manure really does help to get easily assimilated plant food into the soil so as to lead to proper development and the production of many blooms.

Never over feed, for if this is done it will lead to coarse growth and the possible breakdown of plant tissues and the susceptibility to disease. In checking up the analysis of any feeding agent employed, it should be remembered that Geraniums prefer a slightly alkaline soil, and although nitrogen is essential for proper development and colouring of the foliage, too much causes unwanted growth. Potash, phosphates and calcium are all needed in a balanced form, and this is why it is particularly sensible to mix bone meal and decayed manure with the compost used, since they gradually release the vital properties required by the plants in a way that they most easily assimilate them, and their proper use greatly lessens the possibility of an unbalanced growth and disease.

Perhaps one of the most undesirable things which occurs with Geraniums permanently grown in pots, is the algæ or green growth which frequently develops on the outside of the receptacles, which prove detrimental to the appearance of the plants whether in the greenhouse, living room or when being sent to the market. It has been the practice of commercial growers and others to get rid of the algæ which occurs on pots in greenhouses, by spraying with one of the copper compounds.

This cannot wholeheartedly be recommended, however, since such spraying does retard normal root development and in some cases has led to definite injury to plant life, and at the best, the upset of the roots by the solution working its way through the walls of the pots makes it perhaps best to avoid these copper solutions.

For the average small grower, the safest way of keeping the outside of the pots clean, is to give them occasional rubbings over with soap and water.

4

BEDDING OUT

THAT the Geranium is suitable for bedding purposes is well illustrated by the fact that it was so widely used and for so long, during the Victoria era, and there are in fact, few subjects to equal it for providing a continuous summer show of really bright colour. What other flower is there that will do so well in smoky industrial areas and which will keep on blooming until frosts prevent its continuance out of doors, and yet which is equally at home in the cleanest city or the remotest country district? Not only so, it is a subject which is always largely depended upon for providing colour for important occasions, and once again the brilliance of the Geranium was in evidence during the last Coronation year, both in town and country areas, brightening the grounds of large companies and the tiny gardens of private houses.

When beds and borders are cleared of bulbs and spring bedding subjects, they can immediately be replanted with Geraniums, which, if they have been treated properly, will be in full growth by the end of May and commencing to produce their succession of showy blooms. They will keep on doing so for the whole time that they are in the garden.

To the surprise of many people varieties could, and still can of course, be found to plant up to form a bed or border of our national colours, and a suggestion in this direction is to use Paul Crampel or Gustav Emich for scarlet, Ryecroft White or Heroine (or Hermoine) for white, and A. M. Mayne for a blue—although the latter is really a purple, another regal colour.

Two charges are frequently made against the Geranium: the first being that the colours are glaring and monotonous, the second that the plant lacks elegance and beauty. Both of these accusations come as a result of an imperfect knowledge of a most useful plant, for there is colour enough in the extremely wide range of varieties available, to prevent any need for employing the most vividly coloured sorts, so that it is unnecessary to be restricted to any one shade of colour.

There is also the objection sometimes raised that, particularly in certain seasons, the plants tend to make too much leaf growth; but if when this is seen to be occurring the growing points are taken out, flower bearing laterals will form and, incidentally, they will keep the plants from becoming weak and spindly looking. Why should one not stop a Geranium in the same way as is done with many other popular garden flowers to keep them shapely and encourage even more flowers to appear?

There are single and double varieties, Zonals and Ivy-leaved sorts, many of the latter being useful as a ground cover as well as for using in raised vases, urns, etc. Some may be grown as standards with one or more stems, while a number of the scented-leaved varieties, with their ornamental foliage, always attract attention when bedded out. It is, however, in the coloured-leaved varieties that such an extensive choice is available, and with practically all of this section, the flowers are small and are often removed so that full appreciation may centre upon the coloured leaves. To mention just a few specially variegated foliaged kinds, particularly suited for bedding and fully described in Chapter XI, the following never fail to prove satisfactory: Caroline Schmidt, Mrs. Pollock, Mrs. Strang, Mrs. Henry Cox, Mrs. Quilter and Marechal Mac-Mahon.

There are a few dwarf-growing varieties particularly suitable for edging purposes. These include the scarce and slow-growing Black Vesuvius, Golden Hieover and the most unusual Madame Salleroi, which has a silver edge to the light green leaves.

The range of Zonals is really extensive, and although the scarlet Paul Crampel is nowadays often ignored, it remains a highly dependable, free-flowering sort which will put up with much bad treatment and neglect and yet continue to produce its blooms in profusion. Even so, the now popular variety Gustav Emich is often grown in preference. It is of a rather lighter colour than Paul Crampel and equally as free flowering, holding its flowers on stiff stems well above the foliage. It is a strong grower, so much so that in damp weather it needs to be frequently stopped to keep the rampant growth under control.

As a salmon-orange Maxim Kovaleski needs a lot of beating, its sturdy blooms being most attractive. King of Denmark and Mrs. Lawrence are reliable light pinks. Notting Hill Beauty is officially described as geranium-lake, and has the desirable quality of hardly ever being out of flower during the summer. The single cherry-red Doris Moore, one of the newer varieties, always shows up well in beds and borders. Henry Jacoby, of which there are both single and double forms, was grown many years before the famous Paul Crampel was known and is still among the best—proof enough of the reliability; its colour is deep red. As a change, and provided it is used with discretion, Belvedere Glory, a sport from Paul Crampel, is worth growing. Its colour is a shade of magenta-pink, and so must be planted where it will not clash with other plants being bedded out. There are one or two good varieties of a purple shade, including George Burgwin, single, and Madame Hibbault, double; but, although sometimes recommended for bedding, I have found that A. M. Mayne produces such large flower heads that they are inclined to bend over or become broken after rain or winds, and for that reason alone other varieties should be used.

The majority of the Ivy-leaved sorts, too, are well worth using for bedding, either on their own or in conjunction with other subjects. All of the varieties in this section are of rather prostrate habit if not supported, although the hybrid Ivies are not so straggly. This includes the semi-doubles Achievement, salmon; Lady Gertrude, pink; and the double Millfield Gem, very pale pink with central blotch. Of the older, true Ivy-leaved sorts, La France, lilac, maroon markings; Madame Crousse, pale pink-veined maroon; Charles Turner, double pink-feathered maroon; and Sir Percy Blakeney, double crimson-scarlet, are good. As a deep scarlet, Decorator deserves greater popularity, for it is a good grower and retains its colour well.

Although the singles usually flower more freely than the

doubles, in exposed or windy places, the doubles will be found more satisfactory, since the greater solidarity of their blooms prevents the petals being shattered so easily as the singles.

Never be persuaded that Geraniums can only be grown in beds by themselves, as is sometimes asserted, for this is not correct. They may be mixed with other subjects, although, of course, due regard must then be paid to the other plants, so that suitable companions may be grouped together and so that one does not smother the other or the colours clash. This, of course, applies to all types and varieties.

Although we would not suggest that Geraniums are ideal for planting in shady places, as an experiment certain varieties, including Paul Crampel and Maxim Kovaleski, were planted in the full shade of some plum and apple trees, where it was quite dry and where little else seemed able to grow. There the plants seemed to settle down from the beginning and make a most delightful show, brightening up a prominent place in the garden which would otherwise have been entirely devoid of colour. This has happened for two successive seasons, which admittedly have been rainy ones, but it nevertheless is another point in support of the versatility of the Geranium.

5

PROPAGATION

AMONG the methods of propagation which are open to both the professional and amateur Geranium grower is that of raising plants from seed. It does, however, demand much patience, for it is quite a long process and in any case only quite a small proportion, if any, of the seedlings raised will come true to the type of plant from which the seed was collected. Against this, there is the interest of awaiting results and the possibility (even though extremely slight) of raising a plant with some distinct qualities and one which will be worth perpetuating.

Several specialist growers now offer hand-pollinated seed, in some instances giving the names of the parents from which the seed has come. In some cases crosses have been made by combining likely parents to produce compact growth and particular shades of coloured plants with free-flowering capabilities.

On the other hand, seed pods can be picked from plants of which the flowers have been pollinated through the activity of bees and other insects or by the winds or rains. The Geranium is not a flower which is self-pollinating like, for instance, the Sweet Pea, but is one of a group of plants which are said to have protandrous flowers—that is, the stamens first develop and the little pollen sacs ripen and burst before the stigma or female part of the flowers mature. This naturally means that unless bees, or some other happening, causes pollen to be deposited on the stigma when it has developed and is in a receptive condition, seed cannot form, but that hand pollination is a simple task, especially so since the need for emasculation does not exist.

Even so, when pollen from the finest varieties is used it does not by any means follow that any of the seedlings raised, will make worthwhile new plants. In very many cases the seedlings revert and become similar to the primitive ancestor, and at other times, the flowers which appear are so near to one of the parents, that the plants could not be given another name. Other seedlings will be found to be of poor constitution or have other undesirable characteristics, so that it must be said that the possibility of securing a really tip-top new variety is very remote. However, it is the persistence of the plant breeder that makes him what he is—always an optimist—and since there is always a chance, slight though it may be, that something good will turn up, no real enthusiast will be undaunted when it comes to seeing what he can produce in the way of seedlings, although here, it must be said that to save cluttering up one's greenhouse with seedlings of little merit, it is necessary to be absolutely ruthless in cutting out everything not of the very highest standard.

What, then, is the process by which seeds are obtained? Having selected the parents, remembering that the flower of the female parent should be a day or two in advance of the male parent, it is wise to carefully cover the former with a paper or other thin bag to ensure that no insect or other agent transfers pollen to the receptive stigma.

Some growers have found it an advantage to withhold water from plants just at the fertilising stage, since it seems that very frequently a much better set of seed results under fairly dry root conditions. The selected male parent should be watched so that when the little sacs on the top of the stamens, commonly known as anthers, are ripe and ready to burst, releasing the pollen grains, the latter can be used on the flower selected as the female parent. When the pollen is ready, the protective covering is taken from the female flower and the actual pollinating operation should then be carried out with great care. Mid-morning, or at any rate before noon, seems to be the best time of day for the job, which is most simple, since it only requires the use of a very clean, fine camel-hair brush to transfer most carefully the pollen from the stamens on to the receptive stigma of the female parent. This will be slightly sticky, thus enabling the pollen to adhere easily. Particularly with very special varieties it is wise to re-cover the pollinated flower, the bag being removed when it is seen, normally within a few days, that a little seed pod is forming. Provided pollination has been effective—for, of course, pollinated blooms do not necessarily become fertilised, although most do as soon as the petals fall—the long, pointed seed vessel will quickly take on the shape of a Stork's Bill, which, as already explained, is why the Geranium is sometimes given this name.

Given plenty of light, the seed pod will soon ripen, when the seed can be harvested in the usual way and later may be sown in an attempt to raise something really new and worthwhile, but seed harvested when unripe will prove useless. Even when two parents most likely to produce something very startling are crossed, it is by no means certain that any seedlings of real value will materialise. Frequent examination of the pods is necessary to prevent the seed being lost when the pod splits unnoticed, since the hair spring-like tail on the end unfolds rapidly, causing the seed to be ejected and fall to the ground, often at some little distance from the actual plant. Therefore, when particular crosses have been made, it is wisest to gather the seed pods just before they are quite ripe and place them in a box or other receptacle, and as soon as the first signs of the pod splitting occurs, the seeds can be shaken out into a bag and will be ready for sowing as required, which for best results, should be within a month of gathering. As to the sowing, the little tail should be cut from the seed, most of which will germinate freely, so long as it is fresh when sown, within twelve to fifteen days, although in some cases a very much longer time elapses, so that it is unwise to disturb the compost too soon. It is, of course, necessary to remove seedlings as they become ready for potting up. No elaborate seed-sowing mixture is required and the John Innes seed compost is very suitable, although a simple mixture can easily be made by using any good sifted loam, peat and silver sand, plus, where possible, some fine well-decayed manure.

Artificial fertilisers are best entirely avoided, for they tend to induce rapid top growth without a corresponding root system. Water must be applied as necessary, but if the compost is made and kept too sodden the seed may rot away. Either seed pans or boxes may be used and the seed covered with an eighth of an inch of compost. They should be kept in an even temperature around fifty-five to sixty degrees, and when big enough to handle, the seedlings must be transferred to small pots and then to larger ones as growth proceeds. The period between seed sowing and the seedlings flowering must be one of patience, since it generally means waiting well over a year and sometimes up to eighteen months, before the value of the flowering capabilities of the young plants can be assessed. Sometimes, although a young plant may show evidence of being of great merit, it may have other traits which offset its good qualities, so that it will be for the grower to decide whether it may be possible to outbreed by further selection, any undesirable points and replace them with those which will ensure a plant of real value. It is not worthwhile wasting time on inferior plants but rather to set a high standard and stick to it, otherwise a lot of space becomes taken up with second-rate plants.

A PLANT SPOILED BY TAKING OFF ALL GROWING
POINTS FOR CUTTINGS

PLATE I.
Variegated Pelargonium,
Marechal Macmahon

Photo: J. E. Downward

PLATE II.
Pelargonium (zonal)
King of Denmark.

Photo: J. E. Downward

PLATE III.
Pelargonium Crispum
Variegatum makes an
attractive scented foliage
plant for the greenhouse.

PLATE IV.
Zonal. A well-
balanced free-flowering
variegated Geranium.

Although comparatively few Geranium growers go in for raising plants from seed, a very large quantity of plants are propagated from cuttings. This is not to be wondered at, for, as has already been said, by the seed method many months must elapse before a flowering-size plant is secured, whereas from cuttings, a really good, well-rooted flowering plant can be secured in about two months. Furthermore, one can be sure that by propagating by cuttings the new plants secured will be identical in every way to the plants from which the cuttings were taken—a most important point when desiring to perpetuate a variety with special qualities. With large-growing plants the taking of cuttings will do more than provide a good stock of young plants, for it will, if the cuttings are carefully removed, keep the parent plants of good shape and prevent the development of elongated specimens with woody, crowded stems.

Theoretically the best plants are obtained from the tops or growing points of the stems, for normally the strongest, liveliest activity is there. The length of the cuttings should be about three inches with about three joints. It is hardly necessary to say that cuttings should not be taken from plants which do not flower or those which appear to have any undesirable characteristics.

There is perhaps no actual closed season for taking cuttings, but undoubtedly the majority are secured in August and September, usually when stock plants are being prepared for their winter quarters, in many cases being brought in from outdoor beds. Cuttings taken in the autumn will need slight heat during the winter, and by the following May and June will normally prove to be fully capable of producing a good supply of bloom throughout the whole of the summer. February and March are other good months, too, for securing cuttings, which under ordinary cultivation will become well rooted in about three weeks after being inserted. Very often these cuttings will prove to be almost as satisfactory in the way of early blooms as autumn-struck cuttings.

Whilst cuttings can be made in every other month it is really best to avoid November and December, since then they are more likely to damp off with black rot of the stem. As to the actual selecting and preparing of the cuttings, it is best to avoid excessively soft and sappy growth, for often these are produced on plants which have not been particularly free flowering, and

2

this especially applies in seasons where there has not been much sun to ripen the stems.

The lower leaves and stipules should be removed, but at least two leaves should be left; failure to do this will result in delayed rooting and the risk of damping off.

The old-fashioned practice of leaving the cuttings out of the soil for a few hours after they have been taken is not a sound one, although it was very frequently done on one of the nurseries at which I received my training. It is best to have the compost ready, so that the cuttings can be inserted as soon as they are taken. It is generally supposed that this exposing treatment will cause the freshly severed bottom end of the cutting to become rapidly sealed by the formation of a layer of skin, but the desirable sealing does, of course, form naturally

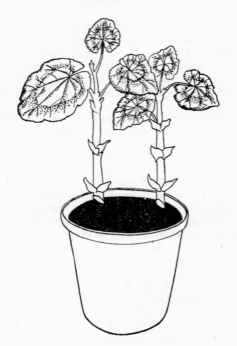

WHERE TO INSERT CUTTINGS AROUND EDGE OF POT

when the cuttings have been inserted in the compost. The only exception to this, is when it is necessary to propagate from very soft cuttings, since then it does seem probable that there is some value in allowing the cut ends to dry by being exposed to the cool air for some time.

Although the modern growth hormones are sometimes recommended to encourage rapid rooting I never use them or consider it necessary to do so, for under ordinary circumstances Geranium cuttings will readily make roots and do not need any stimulus in this connection. If hormones are used, it should be remembered that they are not effective in soils which are rich in lime, for there they are made ineffective by reaction with calcium.

Just here, perhaps, is a good point to say that with the Black Vesuvius Zonal varieties, the growth hormones can be of help since these varieties are rather more difficult to root. An additional difference being that cuttings are best secured in the early months of the year, the normal trade practice being to root them on the benches or in pots where there is some bottom heat.

It is essential for good results to make a perfectly clean cut immediately below the node or joint, which means that a really sharp knife is indispensable, for a torn or jagged base will invite the entry of disease, as will the making of a cut in between the joints. It is at the joints that the cell activity is at its greatest and where the roots form most readily. Incidentally, one of the advantages of using a rooting compost containing sand, or of inserting the cuttings in pure sand as is sometimes advised, is that the sand touching the base of the cuttings stimulates them, causing the root "points" to form very quickly after callousing has occurred. With large quantities of cuttings, and where there is the convenience available, the cuttings can be rooted in clean sand or very sandy compost in a frame from which it is possible to exclude frost and maintain a temperature of fifty-five to sixty degrees Fahrenheit. Watering must be done with care. In fact, after an initial good watering to settle the soil firmly around the cuttings, they should be kept rather on the dry side. Seed boxes, too, may be used for the cuttings, but the best method is to use the small so-called thumb pots, for they not only save soil but since the roots work freely into the little pots, when potting on is necessary, there is not the slightest check in growth and the possibility of black leg is minimised.

The plunging of the pots into a bed of peat is a great aid to growth, especially where there is the provision of soil-warming through the use of electric wires.

For the small grower, and where space is limited, the best way of growing on the cuttings is either to insert them singly in small pots or put a number round the edge of a five inch pot. The first potting is done in the sixty or two and a half inch diameter size pots, in which, in the case of autumn-rooted cuttings, the young plants are kept during the winter. The ideal way of keeping young stock during that period is to plunge the pots into sandy soil or peat in a frostproof frame, but since such a facility is not available for the average gardener, it means keeping the plants in the greenhouse or some living-room. There the temperature should centre around fifty-five to sixty degrees Fahrenheit and should never fall below forty degrees. Plenty of light, little water and a rather dry atmosphere should be the aim.

In the early spring it is necessary to pinch out the growing points of the cuttings so as to induce the formation of bushy plants. Do not take too much off, for not only will this tend to delay the proper development of side shoots but it makes the entry of disease easier. As the plant begins to produce flower buds in the spring, a little feeding can be started, but it is again stressed that nitrogenous fertilisers should be applied sparingly.

It is worth saying that success with cuttings comes when they are potted firmly and about an inch or an inch and a half deep, without the soil being rammed around them, for when this occurs both proper drainage and porosity are prevented. This does not mean that the cuttings should be left loose or insecure. Plenty of light should be given, and a good place for the young plants, especially very early spring-secured cuttings, is on the shelves or staging near the glass. Dead leaves should be carefully removed so as to minimise the possible entry of disease, while frequent syringings of clear water will be beneficial. One sometimes sees in municipal parks and other public gardens standard Geraniums with stems of three or more feet, and such specimens provide height and character to certain beds and borders and break them up, giving certain less formal effect.

A standard of this height cannot be obtained in one season, but if the lateral shoots are prevented from developing, the required height will be attained either in two or three years, although only really strong growing sorts are worth training in this way.

Another very infrequently practised method of propagation is grafting, although this is not an operation which can whole-heartedly be recommended to the average grower, for experience has proved that even when done with the utmost care only a very few grafts are successful. The theory and practice of grafting Geraniums is the same as for other plants and trees. That is, where a certain variety on its own roots is naturally a poor grower, is shy flowering or has some other undesirable trait, it will usually show very great improvements on such weaknesses when grafted on to another suitable stock variety, and, of course, all buds produced below the grafting point must be removed. Few, if any, amateurs are likely to go in for grafting except as an isolated experiment, so that it is not necessary to go more deeply into the matter in this little volume.

When dealing with older plants which it is desired to keep after they have been lifted from the open ground in the early autumn, especially those which are three or more years old, it is wise to root prune. This is a simple operation and merely consists of carefully cutting off the long roots before potting up for the winter, and both the Zonal and Regal varieties will benefit from this treatment.

Although not always convenient because of lack of space, it is really best to keep selected stock plants growing apart from those bedded out, for it is easier to be certain that a disease-free, true to name stock, is being perpetuated.

It must not be thought that all new varieties are the result of cross fertilisation or hybridising, for there have been many cases of sports or mutations in Pelargoniums, and in fact they are always likely to appear, and frequently do, although only the most obvious ones are noticed. Sometimes they are definitely worth saving and propagating so as to work up a stock. If as the result of such treatment a sport remains true in every way and does not revert and has qualities which make it desirable, stock can be increased vegetatively as necessary.

It seems certain that the first double Zonal, raised in France over ninety years ago, first appeared as a sport, and this happening was certainly a great event in the history of the Geranium, for it was the appearing of this first double that has en-

abled hybridists to produce the many double and semi-double
varieties which are in cultivation to-day. It was, of course,
necessary for the first double to be recognised as a definite
break, and this is why it is always wise to take notice of any
sport, or in fact any plants raised from seed, which are different, just in case they may be further breaks of value.

There are still several colours which are desirable in Zonal
Geraniums, and we all look for the coming of a real yellow and
a pure blue. There are, of course, blue-mauve mauves, which
are sometimes referred to as blue, but so far there is not any
really true blue Zonal. This is another reason why the growing of Pelargoniums is always both interesting and rewarding.

It is well to remember that flowers of some double sorts
appear to be sterile while others seem loath to set seed. There
is also the question of incompatibility among Geraniums to be
considered. It certainly does exist, although there is not a lot
of information available concerning it at the present time.
Another point particularly affecting the double and semi-double
varieties is the greater possibility of the damping off of the seed
heads since they do sometimes retain the moisture which makes
it easier for the grey mould fungus to get a hold. This is
another reason why it is always essential for there to be a
buoyant, fresh atmosphere in the greenhouse. A dusting of
yellow sulphur powder will normally check any tendency towards the start or development of grey mould, provided of
course the powder is used before the disease gets a real hold.

Generally speaking, it is not difficult to propagate most of
the hardy Geraniums. Any which seed fairly freely, such as
G. *Argenteum, erianthium* and *Sanguineum* and its forms, can
have their seed gathered when ripe and either sown then, in a
warm sheltered place, or it can be sown in pots in gentle heat
in February. A good sweet compost is suitable, and in the
case of *Argenteum* a sprinkling of lime added to the soil,
will be appreciated by the seedlings as soon as they begin to
develop.

Healthy established plants may be divided in September or
early October or again in March, the carefully made divisions
being either potted up or planted direct into flowering quarters, except in the case of autumn divisions or where the per-
manent site is inclined to be exposed or damp. Then, early
spring open ground planting is best.

Although hardly ever necessary, cuttings of new season's growth can be taken in July and dibbled in under a shaded frame or cloche, and, in addition, the species *Sanguineum*, *Subcaulescens* and their varieties can be increased by root cuttings. These need only be quite small, say about an inch long and no more than an eighth or a sixth of an inch in diameter.

6

GERANIUMS FOR DECORATION

FOR too long the Geranium as a cut flower for decorative purposes has been kept in the background; this, of course, is for lack of a lead in this connection. Now, however—chiefly through the activities of the lively Geranium Society—more use of cut Geranium flowers for decoration is being made. In this all lovers of the flower can help, for certain varieties, including the so-called Rosebud varieties, can be used by ladies for their personal adornment, and it should be remembered that when picked young and just opening, and with a tiny spot of florists' gum dropped into the base of the petals, the flowers will retain their freshness and charm for many hours. The right sized small heads of flowers can be tucked into the hair and a suitable shade of colour can be selected to match almost any sort or shade of make-up. They can also be worn as sprays with green or variegated foliage. The leaves of Caroline Schmidt, which are grey-green with straw-coloured edges; Harry Hieover, gold with bronze zone; and Flower of Spring, lavender-green, pale yellow edge, are all useful for this purpose. As for the flowers to go with them, what could be better than those rose-like varieties Pink Rambler and Red Rambler, which are included in the Rosebud Geraniums referred to above?

They look well, too, in many of the modern floral decorations. In her book, *How to do the Flowers*, Mrs. Constance Spry includes a delightful photograph in which Regal Pelargoniums are used in conjunction with lily of the valley, irises, lilac and dicentra to form an effective yet simple display.

Oddly enough, although I think it was unintentional, all of these flowers are those which for a time, fell into disfavour but which are now coming greatly into demand, both by the professional florist and the housewife who is keen on flower arrangements in the home and on trying her hand at entering some of the classes staged at flower shows everywhere.

Without difficulty it is possible to make very lovely flower arrangements for the greater part of the year. This, of course, is because of the continuous flowering capabilities of some of the Zonal and Regal varieties. Flowers from the two sections go very well together, since the light, delicate, rather spreading habit of the latter give the necessary contrast to the formal-looking solid Zonals, while the Ivy-leaved and Scented-leaved varieties can be included, not particularly on account of the flowers, but rather because of their attractive foliage which can be made to hang into almost any position. All flowers should be cut before they are fully open, and should there be any objection to cutting on account of the removal of part of the stems needed to set off the flowers, there is always the valid argument that such shoots, if carefully taken off, will make cuttings for rooting after they have served their purpose as part of the floral decoration!

Geraniums have also been seen in fashionable places of late years, being used for the decoration of public halls and have been carried by bridesmaids at weddings. In most cases they have been included in the bouquets, but in one instance a newspaper reported that bridesmaids carried little baskets packed with Geranium flowers in many shades of pink and red. This surely is an idea which can, and will be, extended by the many lovers of the Geranium. The wide colour range and great varietly of foliage available, will surely help to increase the cult of such a remarkable and adaptable plant.

A short while ago, when acting as judge at a flower show, I saw a charming table decoration consisting entirely of Geranium flowers—almost perfect in its arrangement and for the freshness of the flowers and colour blending. I was not judging the decorative classes but was in a position to be near those who were. It was obvious that the judges in question were somewhat taken aback at the make-up of the table and felt that *Geraniums* could not be favourably compared with sweet peas, roses or annuals, which were the subjects used by other competitors. Obviously they were wrong, and it is this kind of attitude that we Geranium lovers and growers have got to overcome.

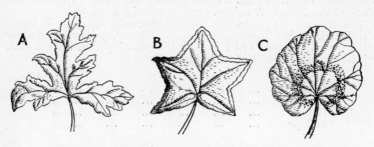

A LEAF OF (A) P. CAPITATUM, (B) P. L'ELEGANTE,
(C) P. MARECHAL MACMAHON

There have also been instances where Geraniums have been most successfully, and with great effect, used in floral tributes, and in one of the bulletins issued by the Geranium Society mention was made of a tribute being formed in the shape of a cushion. Double white Geraniums were used, the blooms being edged with the scented leaves of *Pelargonium Radula*, which provided an effective background. In one corner was placed a spray of double Jacoby flowers with a little asparagus fern to set them off. As was reported, the wreath in question caused much interest, and many who saw it and who enquired the name of the flowers used were rather incredulous when told they were just Geraniums!

Fortunately, many flower show organisers are now including more classes for Geraniums in their show schedules, and where such are still not provided for, every effort should be made to ensure that classes are included both for cut blooms and pot plants. The Royal Horticultural Society has recently published the Horticultural Show Handbook, which replaces the old Rules for Judging issued by the same authority. It is pleasing to see that due regard has been given to the Geranium, and as a guide to enable would-be exhibitors to become familiar with the official standards set for the plant, the following extract of the official pointing system is reprinted with the permission of the R.H.S.

PELARGONIUMS, IVY-LEAVED

Meritorious: A floriferous plant of pleasing form. Ample, healthy, clean and bright foliage. Trusses which are fully expanded and clear of the foliage. A bright, clear and decided colour.

Defective: A plant which is of unpleasing form, or is partly defoliated, or has insufficient flowers. Coarse, yellowing, dull or dirty leaves. Trusses which are not fully developed or are not clear of the foliage. A dull or undecided colour.

						Points.
Plant	...	...	...	...	...	... 8
Trusses	...	...	...	...	...	... 4
Colour	...	...	...	...	...	... 4
Foliage	...	...	...	...	...	... 4
						——
						20

PELARGONIUMS, ZONAL AND REGAL

Meritorious: A shapely plant, bearing trusses of flowers proportionate in number to its size. Ample, healthy and clean foliage. Large trusses, with flowers arranged neither too closely nor too thinly, borne on strong stems clear of the foliage. Large, round flowers, with broad, overlapping petals. Bright, clear and decided colours.

Defective: A misshapen or partly defoliated plant, with too few trusses for its size. Leaves which are coarse, yellowing or dirty. Trusses which are small, thin, or have too few fully expanded flowers, or have weak stems, or stems which do not hold the flowers clear of the foliage. Flowers which are small or have narrow petals. Dull or undecided colours.

						Points.
Plant	...	...	...	...	...	... 5
Trusses	...	...	...	...	...	... 4
Form of flower	...	...	...	...	...	... 3
Colour	...	...	...	...	...	... 5
Foliage	...	...	...	...	...	... 3
						——
						20

The above allocation of points have met with some criticisms on the part of the Geranium Society, of which the members of the Show Committee have given considerable attention to the matter. As a result, the following slightly modified allocation of points will be used by the Society in connection with its own shows, although no doubt individual judges, working apart from the Society, will follow the R.H.S. pointing system.

Classes.	Plants.	Trusses.	Form of Flowers.	Colour.	Foliage.
ZONALS					
Single, semi-double, double	5	4	3	5	3
Cactus and rose-bud	5	4	5	3	3
Miniatures ...	8	3	3	2	4
IVY-LEAF					
Normal and hybrid	8	3	3	2	4
VARIEGATED					
Zonal and Ivy-leaf	10	—	2	—	8
SCENTED	10	—	2	—	8
REGALS	5	4	3	5	3

So many people nowadays are saying and showing that they like Geraniums and intend to grow them, that the future of the plant seems well assured. The last show of the Geranium Society in London attracted an increased number of entries in the competitive classes, while the trade displays make it quite evident that the specialist firms were helpful in fostering interest, both by the way in which they staged the exhibits and the tremendously wide range of varieties shown, including many which have for years been difficult to find.

It is not essential to exhibit an unusual variety; in fact, some of the well-known sorts will always look well on the show bench provided they are properly grown and shown. As far as possible, plants which carry well-balanced spikes with large, bright, clean florets should be staged. Great care will be necessary in getting the plants to the place of exhibition, for the petals can be so easily damaged or knocked off, and unless the show schedule states otherwise, the doubles and semi-doubles are quite as eligible as the singles.

7

HANGING BASKETS AND WINDOW BOXES

ONCE widely used in all parts of the country, hanging baskets, which have been out of favour for many years, are again becoming popular, and undoubtedly they will be much in evidence during coming years.

Such baskets look delightful in porchways or overhanging verandas. In addition, they are sometimes used very effectively by town councils or other public bodies for street decoration, although draughty places should be avoided.

Perhaps the most important point in securing entirely satisfactory results is to line the basket with moss or similar material which will keep the soil within the basket and give a firm base for the plants used. For soil, the John Innes compost is very suitable, and especially so if a saucer containing charcoal is placed in the basket before any soil is added. It is important to ensure that the hook or support used will stand the weight of the filled basket, which is really heavy after it has been watered.

In this connection it is not satisfactory to water the hanging basket with a water-can, for then the moisture will just run off. It is far better to immerse the whole basket in a bath or pail until it is well soaked. Then allow it to drain off before returning the basket to its proper place.

There are many interesting and showy summer- and autumn-flowering plants which can be used, and for trailing subjects the Ivy-leaved Geraniums are invaluable, especially Charles Turner and Galilee, used either by themselves or combined with *Asparagus Sprengeri*, tradescantia, trailing lobelia, nepeta, periwinkles, nasturtiums, *Linaria Cymbalaria*—all are most useful.

Since for hanging baskets it is essential to select plants which have a long period of bloom, the Zonal Geraniums are easily the first choice, for under ordinary circumstances they will flower outdoors from the end of May until October. Such varieties as Paul Crampel, Gustav Emich and King of Denmark seem able to withstand all the vagaries of our summer weather, including winds which shrivel most other subjects.

While various kinds of baskets may be employed, the wire

type is certainly the cheapest, an added advantage being that plants such as *Helxine Solierolii* or *Selaginella* can be worked in among the moss used for lining. Do not make the mistake of finishing off the basket with a mound of soil, for this makes proper watering impossible.

Window boxes give opportunity of growing many more plants than hanging baskets, since their size is only governed by the length of the window sill. They should never be less than six inches wide, and a much better effect can be secured where the width is at least nine inches. Depth, too, is important, and anything less than eight inches does not allow sufficient space for the necessary drainage material and soil.

All window boxes must be strong and well constructed, and it is essential for them to be entirely secure so as to exclude any possibility of accidents due to the boxes or soil falling. The inside of the box is best treated with one of the timber preservatives, but on no account use creosote, which is fatal to plant life. The exterior of the box, too, should have a couple of coats of good paint. Metal boxes are often used, but they sometimes get very hot in summer.

If an inner lining can be obtained, this is invaluable, for it can be lifted out of the box proper and is useful for watering purposes and for replenishing the box with fresh plants when necessary. Whatever receptacle is used must have drainage holes and adequate material placed at the bottom to assist the getaway of surplus moisture. The John Innes compost is suitable, although extra leaf mould is advisable, since it prevents the soil from drying out so quickly.

As regards plants to use, almost all bedding subjects may be put in, but some consideration must be given to the nature and type of the house and surroundings to avoid colour clashes. Certainly bedding Geraniums as recommended for hanging baskets take some beating for window boxes, the Ivy-leaved varieties being specially attractive as they trail over the front of the boxes. To prevent the soil splashing on to the window, cover the visible soil surface with coconut fibre or similar material, and this surface mulch will also conserve soil moisture; an essential point for, although another advantage in favour of, using Geraniums for window boxes is that they will withstand drought, where an even supply of moisture is available, the plants will continue to produce healthy growth and an abundance of blooms of first-rate quality.

Perhaps a further word regarding varieties of Geraniums to use should be given, for although the sorts already mentioned are well-tried, dependable favourites, any effect made to provide a wider colour range than the usual pinks and reds will be well repaid.   In this connection, many of the variegated foliaged sorts can be employed.   Among the best of these for the purpose of providing arresting colour combinations is Mrs. Quilter, with its chestnut zone and pink flowers, planted with Galilee, one of the best pink Ivy-leaved varieties; Caroline Schmidt, double scarlet flowers and silver leaves, with one of the scarlet Ivy's such as Sir Percy Blakeney in front; Lady Churchill or Chelsea Gem, with its fine silver leaves and double pink flowers, and the Ivy-leaved, pink-flowered Charles Turner.

Another simple yet effective idea, is to plant up a number of sweet-scented-leaved varieties, for with these there is not only a variety of perfume but a great variation in the colour and shape of the foliage.   This sort of box is perhaps most suitable for the conservatory or the inside of a living-room.   It is well worth repeating, that whatever boxes or baskets are used, regular supplies of moisture are necessary, and an extra quantity of peat or leaf mould added to the growing compost, will help to prevent rapid drying out.

8

WINTER-FLOWERING GERANIUMS

IT is one thing to say that Geraniums will flower in the winter but quite another thing to get them to do so, for although it is not at all difficult to have colour from March until October, for the remaining months more care is necessary.   Even so, provided certain simple precautions are put into operation and the right sorts are depended upon, some Geraniums can be relied upon to produce blooms throughout the shortest days. Furthermore, healthy plants which have given of their best during the dark days will still continue to flower well the following summer without showing any apparent signs of loss of vitality. Also, some of the smaller young plants which have been bedded out during the summer can be potted up for greenhouse work, and many such will flower again after the check of transplanting into the open.

It is best to specially take cuttings with the idea of getting winter-flowering plants. Any amateur who has the means of providing sufficient heat to exclude frost and keep out damp can do this; in fact, a lot of heat is not required, since the plants prefer a pressing, buoyant atmosphere, although of course frosts will destroy the plants. Occasionally a successful show of winter bloom can be had from early autumn-struck cuttings, but best results undoubtedly come from young plants secured in March and April. It is important to take out the growing tips, once the cuttings have rooted, to induce the formation of laterals which makes for a good bushy, free-flowering plant.

Experiments have been made with artificial lighting, and these have certainly proved that some varieties, at least, respond well to such treatment, the foliage usually being a better colour and healthier looking than one normally gets in the winter. This system demands the removal of flower buds during the summer, and an important difference in colouring is the same as that which also occurs with other subjects grown in this way, the blooms often being smaller and the colour paler than when grown naturally.

When many of the now popular winter flowering subjects were unknown, Zonal Pelargoniums occupied an important place in the greenhouse, conservatory or even windows of those who required colour during the darkest days of the year, but the introduction of many other types of winter-flowering plants has led to the neglect of Pelargoniums for this purpose.

Growing plants under artificial lighting is not likely to be carried out by the average Geranium grower, so that there is no need to go into further detail here.

It is really only worth while trying to get the Zonals to bloom in the winter; the other sections seem most shy to do so, and even with the Zonals, care should be taken in selecting the varieties. The following, fully described in the chapter on varieties, have all proved to be reliable for flowering during the shortest days of the year: F. V. Raspail, which is smallish growing and of wiry appearance, Caroline Schmidt, Decorator, Double Henry Jacoby, Notting Hill Beauty, Gustav Emich, Victory, Lady Warwick and Paul Crampel.

Regular ventilation, plenty of light and the removal of dead leaves are essentials, and although water should be given as necessary, to keep the plants in good condition, it must be kept down to the minimum, for with the fairly low winter temperatures there is always a greater possibility of mildew or decay setting in should excessive moisture be given. It is a mistake to overpot, for although one obviously wants to obtain plants as large as possible for winter flowering, much root room will encourage leaf and stem growth at the expense of flowers. Geraniums flower most freely in the winter when they are more or less pot-bound and the stems have slightly hardened, and a really good show can be secured from plants in four and five inch diameter pots. Sometimes, where larger plants are available to begin with, they can be put into bigger receptacles, especially if they have a good-sized root system. Young plants should, however, be in their actual flowering size pots not later than early October. The John Innes Potting Compost No. 2 will prove to be a most suitable rooting medium, or a simple mixture of three parts fibrous loam, one part peat and half part silver sand with a dusting of hoof and horn or bone meal will be found ideal. Additionally, a little mortar rubble or brick dust will be of great benefit.

It is also worth while giving each plant, in the late autumn, a pinch of fish manure or some other good organic fertiliser. This is far better than any attempt to feed with one of the forcing, quick-acting fertilisers, which may bring the plants into bloom quickly but which will rapidly weaken and exhaust them.

9

SOME RELIABLE ZONAL VARIETIES

THE recent Geranium revival has meant the increased propagation of very many little-grown varieties and brought to light many more. It would be quite impossible to describe or even mention all varieties worth growing, so that in a handbook such as the present one, we must content ourselves in referring to varieties which are both well worthy of cultivation and which are actually available, although some may need seeking for.

This means, of course, that many good varieties will of necessity have to be omitted, even although they were known and loved by gardeners who grew them so well, up to the very early part of this century. It must not, therefore, be taken for granted that if a variety is not mentioned, that it is necessarily faulty or not worthy of consideration. Neither is it to be inferred that all varieties are reliable for outdoors. Sorts specially recommended for this purpose are mentioned in the chapter on Bedding Out Geraniums, which will simplify the matter. All are grouped under their respective colour sections.

ZONAL GERANIUMS OF MERIT

Red, Scarlet, Crimson and Rose

Beatrix Little. A recent introduction, making a lovely plant up to eight inches high, with very effective single scarlet flowers, freely produced.

Caroline Schmidt. Double scarlet flowers, silver variegated foliage.

Decorator. A really first-class semi-double crimson-scarlet, a strong grower and excellent for bedding.

Doris Moore. A well-tried, reliable cherry-red variety.

Dryden. Free flowering, the scarlet-red flowers having darker lower petals.

Captain Flayelle. An excellent bedder with large crimson-scarlet flowers of good quality.

Elizabeth Cartwright, A.M., R.H.S., 1950. Carmine red with small white eye. Very suitable for bedding and greenhouse work.

F. V. Raspail. A long-known and reliable sort, with double scarlet flowers which last well. A small grower, but admirable for bedding purposes.

Gustav Emich. An old variety of great value, which has become widely known as the Buckingham Palace Geranium on account of its being planted extensively on the gardens near the Palace. The semi-double scarlet blooms, are continuous in their appearance.

Golden Harry Hieover. Golden-zoned foliage, single red blooms.

Henry Jacoby Double. Another old favourite with dark red flowers.

Mrs. Eddowes. Large; deep velvety red with orange shading and a small white eye.

Millfield Rival. Strong growing, producing giant heads of rose pink.

Paul Crampel. The best known scarlet. Reliable in every way.

Red Black Vesuvius. Must be included here, for although it is dwarf, growing only about six inches high, it produces its showy scarlet blooms in great quantities and has very dark, almost black, foliage.

Ryecroft Pride. One of the very best deep crimson sorts.

Victorius. This is really an extra large, very fine form of Paul Crampel.

Pink, Salmon and Rose

Audrey. Good-sized trusses of semi-double, soft rose-pink.

Barbara Hope. Soft rich pink, shapely plants.

Chelsea Gem. Referred to under the variegated leaved sorts. An effective bedding variety with pale pink flowers.

Dot Slade. Soft salmon rose, single, greenhouse variety.

King of Denmark. Deservedly popular, with large trusses of semi-double salmon pink, on sturdy, short-jointed plants.

Lady Ellenden. Large semi-double, shiny rose-pink.

Mrs. Lawrence. Similar to the former sort but darker.

Mrs. E. G. Hill. Single, bright satin-pink, good for bedding.

Millfield Rival. Strong growing, clear pink with white eye.

Notting Hill Beauty. Most free flowering, rosy scarlet.

Princess of Wales. Rather small, single salmon-pink blooms, strong growing.

Queen of Denmark. A darker shade and stronger-growing King of Denmark.

Salmon Paul Crampel. Forming very large trusses.

The Speaker. A fine semi-double salmon-pink, first class for bedding.

Orange and Orange Salmon

Maxim Kovalesky. A fine bright single orange, which keeps its colour well. Ideal for bedding and a good sort for winter blooming.

Queen of Italy. A delightful single salmon-pink. Extremely free flowering and makes a good pot plant of excellent shape.

Sansovino. A strong grower with large single orange flowers.

Victory. Similar to Paul Crampel but has coppery salmon blooms.

Willingdon Gem. A fine orange with a white eye. Excellent for greenhouse.

Mauve, Purple and Magenta

A. M. Mayne. Double purple-crimson, a strong grower. Sometimes listed as Purple Emperor and A. Magni.

Belvedere Glory. Magenta-pink, otherwise not unlike Paul Crampel.

Brooks Purple. Double magenta-purple of good form.

Festiva Maxima. Double purple of excellent form. Sometimes said to be the same as A. M. Mayne, although some blooms at least, lack the crimson shading, resulting in a really fine purple.

Lord Curzon. Large purple-magenta flowers with white eye.

White, and White and Pink

Hermoine, or Heroine. A double white which is first class for bedding, although occasionally the flowers become lightly stained with pink, excepting when grown indoors, when they are pure white.

Queen of Whites. A fine bedder which freely produces clear white single flowers, with showy yellow stamens.

Lady Warwick. White with edge of deep pink and dependable for winter flowering in the greenhouse.

Ryecroft White. A well-tried reliable double.

While it can be said that Paul Crampel is still the best known and a quite reliable variety, it is often spoken of very slightingly nowadays. The colour is certainly rather flamboyant, which perhaps is why Gustav Emich is sometimes preferred for bedding and pot work, but a variety which has stood the test of time as Paul Crampel has, for it is over fifty years since it was first introduced from Nancy in France by the man whose name it bears, undoubtedly has many good qualities which cannot be destroyed, either by ignoring it or choosing some other variety instead. It is a pity that many seedlings of the variety have been retained and grown on, some being offered as Paul

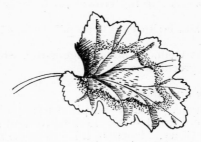

LEAF OF *Pelargonium Zonale* SPECIES

Crampel, whereas they are not at all like the true variety in habit or colour, while others have been renamed often without justification. Not infrequently does one see offered plants labelled Paul Crampel which are very definitely not that variety, and recently I saw a large batch of plants so named which had very small red flowers and foliage without any trace of zoning. It is evident that the variety offered was wrongly named, but did the purchasers know, and did they find out that these plants failed to come up to the standard claimed for Paul Crampel, and so feel they had justification for saying that the variety has deteriorated or "run out"? The maxim is, of course, always purchase plants from reliable specialist growers and so be sure of getting correctly named sorts.

The fact that Gustav Emich received a R.H.S. Award of Merit only a few years ago, has made many people believe that it is a new variety. This is certainly not so, for it has been in cultivation getting on for fifty years, being one of the good scarlets which were much employed for bedding and pot work. Originally it did not gain a lot of appreciation, although it has always been a variety which has held its petals better than many singles, and this is one reason why it is now often used in preference to Paul Crampel.

Some American growers now offer the Zonal Geraniums as two distinct types, the standard and the French or Bruant. The former is the original race of Zonals from the well-known parents *Pelargonium Zonale* and *P. Inquinans*, and is typified in such examples as Maxim Kovalesky and Mrs. Lawrence. The first of the Bruant types, which take their name from a French hybridist, first apeared in France as apparently, a breakaway from the standard type, about 1880.

These are more vigorous in growth and have leaves which are larger, coarser and with more serrated edges. The flower stems are thick, while the irregular flowers have stronger petals which do not fall so rapidly as those of the older Zonals.

They are therefore very suitable for potting, while they are most free flowering when grown in pots. In addition, the long-lasting qualities of the flowers make them useful for cutting and general decoration. Not apparently available in this country in quantity as yet, there is every reason to believe that they will be before long and that they will soon become quite popular.

How the famous Zonal Geranium Paul Crampel was intro-duced is rarely told. Just over fifty years ago, the man whose name this variety bears was a nurseryman at Nancy, France. In a batch of seedlings there appeared an unusual-looking

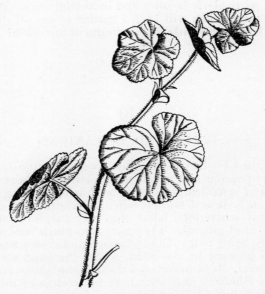

Pelargonium inquinans

plant which obviously showed great possibilities, and being a shrewd man, Paul Crampel did not take long to assess its value.

He built up a large stock from the one plant, although it is said that he did not reveal what he was doing to any of his employees or anyone else, and took great pains in keeping the plants under his personal supervision, carefully keeping the flower buds regularly removed before they showed colour, lest someone should guess his find and some of his plants would be missing.

He sold many plants for twenty shillings or more each, so that it did not take long to make a very handsome sum of money. This same variety is to-day still really important, especially where clean, virus-free stocks are grown, and one should always insist on having the true sort and not some other light scarlet which is frequently distributed as Paul Crampel.

In spite of all that has been said during the last few decades against this variety, it is very doubtful whether there is any other flowering subject which is so suited for the beds of small gardens, particularly in town and industrial areas. What other plant is there which will keep a garden so gay all the summer at so little cost and with the minimum of attention?

.

10

IVY-LEAVED GERANIUMS

THE so-called Ivy-leaved Geraniums were, like the Zonals, once extremely popular and widely used for window boxes, hanging baskets and ornamental vases, as well as for making attractive displays in beds and borders when associated with other bedding plants, where their habit of growth enables them to cover a good deal of ground. They were also much used as upright specimens, being tied to light supports and grown against walls or fences or even in the open, where the supports kept the growths erect. It is, however, I think, a mistake to refer to this section as climbers, since they have no tendrils or other means of keeping themselves upright, and without a support will always grow horizontally, although they do look attractive when trained on little trellis-work. This, of course, is what makes them so valuable for trailing over ornametal vases or containers, especially those raised to a good height.

The Ivy-leaved varieties withstand a good measure of rough treatment and even neglect and poor soil, and yet give a good display of colour. Besides this, when it is necessary to restrict the growth of the stems, the plants do not object to their growing points being constantly pinched out; in fact, then, it often seems, that the leaves assume an especially clean, glossy, dark green colour and maintain a good shape. Furthermore, it is possible to build up standard plants by training the main growth and removing all the lateral shoots; the plants thus secured can be grown on for several years with great success. In warm parts of France, Spain and North Africa it is possible to see good healthy specimens growing several feet in height. In Britain it always pays to take a supply of cuttings annually and so have a regular flow of young plants coming to maturity.

As to the origin of this class of Pelargonium, it descends from the two species *Pelargonium Peltatum* and *P. Hederæfolium*, which is a clear indication of why the Ivies, with their shield or ivy-shaped leaves, are so named. The stems of this section are thinner, harder and longer-jointed than the Zonals. Another difference is that whereas the latter will keep on throwing flower spikes in rapid succession, the Ivy-leaved sorts seem to produce a lot of blooms at one time, when the plants are literally covered with colour, and then have a short rest, afterwards producing another great profusion of flower heads. The normal flowering season is from the end of March until October, the plants being bedded out in the open in June and taken under cover again in September, the exact time depending upon the season. Even when out of flower the plants remain ornamental on account of their glossy green, attractively shaped leaves, While they will sometimes flower during the winter, they cannot be depended on at all for this purpose.

Varieties, as always, must be a matter of personal choice, and although few of the really older sorts are now available, those which are still in cultivation, remain as reliable as they ever were, and with some of the newer varieties, make it possible to secure a very wide range of desirable colours. As far as I am aware, the only variegated Ivy-leaved Geranium obtainable today is the variety L'Elegante, which is the remainder of a small section of coloured-leaved Ivies. The creamy edging to the dark green, shapely leaves, gives the plant a striking appearance and makes it most outstanding, whether grown singly or grouped with other varieties. If the plants are put outdoors during the summer and are kept in low temperatures, the leaves have a tendency to assume a violet-mauve hue, and it is sometimes asserted that the leaves emit a faint but pleasant perfume if they are rubbed or bruised. The whitish flowers are often shaded blush and feathered with reddish-purple markings.

Of the more usual sorts which are altogether dependable, there are Abel Carriere, a large flowered double, light purple; Alice Crousse, double, deep magenta; Galilee, well known and a great favourite for bedding, with rose-pink flowers; La France, with freely produced lilac flowers, feathered maroon; Madame Crousse, another dependable variety, largely used for window boxes and in baskets for street and public building decoration, where the light silvery-pink flowers show up to advantage; Sir Percy Blakeney is another excellent bedder, with double, rich crimson-scarlet flowers; and equally good is the popular Charles Turner, of which the double deep pink flowers are feathered maroon.

Other lesser-known, but reliable sorts, are Dr. A. Chipault, red cerise; Blue Peter, generally believed to be synonymous with Eulalia, and having distinct, double rosette-like flowers of deep mauve; General Clapionette, bright red; Jeane D'Arc, single, white marked lilac; King Edward VII is a really fine, big, rich reddish cerise, semi-double; while Her Majesty The Queen is a pretty single salmon-pink; Leopard is a very large and most arresting sort, the semi-double lilac-pink flowers being blotched crimson on the upper petals; Lord Baden Powell, although old, is a fine variety and is another semi-double, the large blush-lilac blooms having darker featherings; Mauve Beauty is double mauve, the bloom being reminiscent of a rambler rose; while Mrs. W. A. R. Clifton is notable for its choice double scarlet blooms. Of course there are many others available, but those mentioned are among the very best varieties, with a wide colour range.

Even so, mention must be made of the hybrid Ivy-leaved sorts, which are the result of crossing Zonals with the Ivy-leaved Geraniums. This has brought about a little group of varieties having many of the good points of both parents. Equally good for bedding purposes, hanging baskets or individual pot specimens, and among the best of the sorts readily obtainable at the

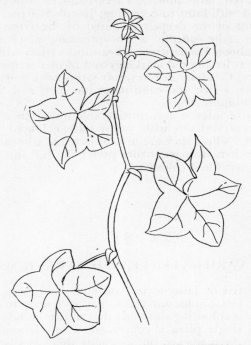

AN UNPREPARED IVY-LEAVED CUTTING

present time, are the following: Achievement, semi-double, salmon-pink flowers, produced on large trusses; Lady Gertrude, another semi-double, with purplish pink heads; Millfield Gem, probably the best of the section, being a strong grower and having very pale blush-pink flowers with a maroon blotch; and Mrs. Hamilton, of robust habit, with large semi-double charming scarlet blooms.

There are quite a number of varieties now freely offered in American catalogues which appear to be highly valuable. Since I have not yet grown or seen them, I mention only a few without comment: Intensity, outstanding, large, deep orange-scarlet flowers; Emily Sylvia, a bright-coloured single, of deep rosy red with orange flush; Willy, really an old sort, with extra double very dark red, large flowers, a free bloomer; Bridesmaid, very soft orchid with faint rose veining; Joseph Warren, rich violet-purple, one of the deepest coloured of the Ivies; Judy, free blooming, cerise purple, a low-spreading plant and a fine grower; Salmon Enchantress, a beautiful variety with large soft pink flowers having red markings and picotee stripes of rose on petal edges; Comtesse de Grey, soft satiny pink flowers, marked light violet, a free and continuous bloomer; and Mrs. Banks, white with bluish shading.

A point of interest and considerable importance, is the fact that whereas varieties with paler, softer-coloured flowers are best planted where they are not subjected to continuous strong sun, the richer, stronger shades prefer the full sun, when they show up their finest colour tones.

11

VARIEGATED-LEAVED GERANIUMS

THE coloured or fancy-leaved varieties have been called the "show-off" Geraniums, and certainly they live up to their name in that their colouring demands that notice be taken of them, whether a single plant is concerned or an elaborate bedding scheme has been worked out. Among their uses is that of an edging or front groundwork for other summer bedding subjects. They like full sunlight; in fact, the more sun the better, since then, all the full colour tones become prominent, and it is surprising how many shades there are in some of the leaves.

While it is not possible to say how these colour variations first arose, since in the earliest of the Pelargoniums all variegated forms were unknown, it seems certain that originally, at least, the coloured-leaved forms came about as a result of chlorophyll deficiency. Some nurserymen were quick to see that the unusualness of the coloured leaves would make the plants of extra value, and they therefore set to work to raise more varieties. So great was their success that to-day there are sorts, not only with light green and yellow markings, but others which have leaves which are marked or veined with cream and silver, gold, bronze, brown and purple.

For the most part, flowers of the coloured-foliaged sorts are rather small, although Mrs. Parker, which is fully described later, has a really good-sized truss. However, since it is for the foliage that these sorts are grown, blooms are not of the first importance. The bicolour or tricolour leaves are for the most part remarkably blended, and whether kept in the greenhouse all the year or bedded out in the summer, they are most effective, as everyone who has seen them used at Kew or Wisley or in all the larger parks will agree.

Besides this, now that house plants are rapidly gaining in popularity, the wide choice of colour available in the variegated Geraniums, makes them high on the list of no-trouble indoor plants which provide an interesting show for a long time, coupled with an air of old-fashioned romance.

It is true to say that, in common with most variegated plants, the fancy-leaved Geraniums are just a little more difficult to grow than the green-foliaged sorts, and those which show the brightest colours are perhaps slightly weaker in constitution, although this may be due to the rather smaller root system they make. In any case, it is essential for the finest results to provide really sharp drainage, and where plants are permanently kept in pots the receptacles should not be too large, for, if so, too much growth may be made, which often spoils the shape of a plant.

Another important point is that, since the leaves of this type of Geranium are rather thick and yet soft, they are inclined to rot off if kept in an atmosphere which is too close and humid. Seeing it is the newest shoots which are the most colourful, it pays to encourage fresh growth and so enjoy the full benefit of the brightest shades. When a plant is inclined to become too leggy, the growing centre can either be cut back and made into a cutting and potted up or just be pinched back in the usual way. In either case, fresh growth will be stimulated by the stopping of the taller stems. A winter temperature of around sixty degrees Fahrenheit will help to maintain the plants in good healthy condition.

Just about 100 years ago much interest was caused in England regarding plants with variegated foliage and the Geranium in particular. A leading plant raiser at that time, named Peter Greives, was largely instrumental in increasing interest in this type of plant. He published a booklet on Ornamental Foliaged Pelargoniums, which, however, has long since been out of print,

and I have eagerly sought to obtain a copy, but in vain. With
the fresh impetus on Geraniums of all sorts, a number of the
forgotten but beautifully marked varieties are being re-dis-
covered, sometimes growing in old country cottages, and it is
to be hoped that before long, many more of these ancient sorts
will come to light again.

Apart from being grown in pots and borders by themselves,
they may be used to advantage in combination with the ordinary bedding Zonal varieties, and in this connection it is quite
in order, and sometimes advisable, to remove the flowers before
they open, so that attention becomes focused on the foliage
itself.

Before mentioning some of the best varieties of the orna-
mental-leaved sorts, there is a little group of bicolour varieties
known as the Butterfly Geraniums. This is because of the leaf
markings, which seem like a butterfly when in flight. The two
best-known varieties are Crystal Palace Gem, with yellowish
green leaves and an irregular central blotch. This variety was
popular towards the end of the last century and has small single
flowers which are a bright scarlet. Happy Thoughts is a smaller
variety, but the margins of the leaves are green; the central
markings being of yellow. Like most of the Fancy varieties,
they do not make a really large specimen and the leaves themselves, in the case of the Butterfly Geraniums, remain on the
small side, which has always been characteristic of this type.

For easy reference the Fancies may be divided into separate
colour sections, and although there are so many named sorts
still available, only a selection can be mentioned because of lack
of space. Silver-leaved: Flower of Spring is a strong-growing
sort which has been known for nearly 100 years and is still one
of the very best of its colour, with an unusually wide, irregular,
deep ivory border. It carries small single scarlet flowers. Caroline Schmidt has a border of straw-yellow and is unusual for the
large size of its deep cerise flowers and the rather ruffled edges
of its leaves. Chelsea Gem is another good variety, and appears
to be identical with Mrs. or Lady Churchill, the plants being
short jointed with tall, pink flowers. Mrs. Mapping is similar
to Flower of Spring, except that the flowers are white with a
pink shading in the centre. Mrs. Parker is a double rose-pink
and one of the finest of all of the silver-leaved sorts, being
largely used for bedding.

Madame Salleroi is a really old variety, sometimes known as

Dainty. It is very dwarf growing, forming a compact bush of no more than four or five inches high, and is therefore ideal for bedding or as an edging variety. This unusual habit of growth leads to really bushy plants which, as far as is known, do not produce any flowers at all—quite an unusual characteristic for any kind of Pelargonium. It makes a splendid contrast when planted with other dwarf-growing sorts, especially those which have leaves with darker zonings, since the foliage of Madame Salleroi is a glossy silvery green. In old catalogues this variety was sometimes listed as Little Dorrit—quite an appropriate name. Another old variety, similar to Madame Salleroi, of which it is considered to be a sport, is Little Trot, which has rather quaint, small, single, pink flowers, with an attractive silver colouring in the leaves. Included in this section, too, are the two scented-leaved sorts *Crispum Variegatum* and Lady Plymouth, referred to on page 65.

Of the golden-leaved varieties, in addition to Happy Thoughts and Crystal Palace Gem already mentioned, there are a number of others worthy of consideration and well worth hunting for. Golden Crampel is a dwarf with the absence of any zone or markings in the leaves, which no doubt is the reason of it sometimes being known as the Gold Leaf Geranium, the single red flowers, which are freely produced, having a showy white eye. Verona is somewhat similar, although the flowers are pinky-magenta.

There are also some excellent tricolour-leaved sorts, and Mrs. Henry Cox is one of the most widely used. It has really brilliant-hued foliage, which, in addition to the gold colour, contains red, purple and other shades, going on to an almost black tone; a dwarf grower, it produces salmon-pink flowers. Mrs. Pollock, too, finds many admirers, and is largely used in formal beds laid out by public authorities. The flat, deeply serrated leaves are marked with pale gold, purple and red, the flowers being scarlet-vermilion in colour. Very similar is Mrs. Strang, although in this case, the flowers are double cerise and the foliage seems to be particularly bright and showy. Golden Harry Hieover is a splendid free-growing dwarf, golden-leaved and bronzy-red zoned sort, making a dwarf compact, yet bushy, plant of no more than five inches in height and producing constant supplies of vermilion-scarlet flowers, being particularly suitable for edging purposes.

Another interesting variety which commands attention, is the one recently offered by that well-known Geranium specialist Mr. W. A. R. Clifton and named Lass o' Gourie. It has single vermilion flowers and leaves of yellow, irregularly zoned reddish purple and green.

Of the plants on which the leaves have a bronzy zone, Marechal McMahon is probably the best known, its single red flowers being carried on rather thin stems. These, however, are often removed before they open without any loss of display, since the colouring of the leaves is most showy, taking in, apart from the bronze, shades of green, gold, bright and deep red, the actual bronze zone itself, being more prominent as the foliage fully develops.

A silver-leaved tricolour of high merit is Mrs. Burdett Couttes, of which the foliage has shadings of pink and purple, while the flowers are rich red. It is a slow grower and not very easy to propagate, which is probably the reason why it is so expensive to buy at the present time.

Mrs. Quilter, with salmon-pink flowers, having a pale centre, is another dependable variegated form, with gold leaves which are zoned a reddish chestnut colour.

An American variety, Skies of Italy, is a very attractive tricolour, having deeply toothed leaves with yellow edges and zoned with crimson-orange. Here, again, the single flowers are of a vermilion colour. Bronze Beauty, too, is another popular variety on "the other side", with fairly large leaves which have a prominent bronze-red zone. The single flowers are salmon-pink.

A very famous old variety is Red Black Vesuvius, which is really a miniature growing sort, having nearly black leaves with just a trace of green evident. The truss of showy scarlet flowers is carried nicely above the foliage and so provides a pleasing contrast to the colour of the leaves. There is a form known as Salmon Black Vesuvius, which is similar in leaf and habit to the previously mentioned sort, but the flowers are of a showy salmon colour.

Yet another similar variety is Mephistopheles, which is even more heavily zoned black and rather stronger growing than Red Black Vesuvius. Quite different is Black Douglas, which is an altogether bright variety, the gold-coloured leaves having a wide bronzy zone. It makes good growth and produces single salmon-pink flowers. Another unusual sort is Distinction, which has lively green foliage and a sharply divided black zone on each leaf, the zone or ring being nearer the edge than is usual. The plant is of dwarf habit and carries red flowers, which show up well.

A variety which is unusual in another way is Mrs. G. Clark, since it not only has pale green leaves but peculiar white stems, which is a characteristic of another little-known sort, Turtle's Surprise.

If only one could refer to catalogues issued early this century it is certain that many more most interesting coloured-foliaged varieties would be found fully described. Even so, although this is not possible, it is surprising how many of the really old sorts have survived, which is an indication of their real worth, for their survival is surely a proof that they refuse to be ousted by new creations, however good and attractive they may be.

Some of the very best of the old sorts may even now be growing on remote cottage window-sills or in conservatories, where old-fashioned subjects are valued and where they await our discovery.

12

SCENTED-LEAVED GERANIUMS

FOR hundreds of years the scented-leaved Geraniums have been favourites among all classes of people. This is not surprising in view of their ease of culture and the great variety of the decorative foliage, coupled with the tremendously wide range of scents available. Many of the scented-leaved sorts are species, while a large number of others are varieties which have been raised intentionally or have come about as natural hybrids. Although there is a considerable difference in the habit of growth, all are easy to cultivate.

Gardeners of a century ago certainly knew the value of fragrance, for not only were these plants used in conservatories and living-rooms, but they were planted alongside garden walks, where the leaves could be thumbed and the scents enjoyed. In addition, they will always make interesting plants for garden beds, tubs, vases and window boxes. Another point in their favour is that they will thrive in town gardens and will withstand the most casual treatment, although they readily respond to any little extra attention given.

Obviously since the plants with their perfumes are particularly valuable during the winter, they will appreciate good treatment during the summer, so that during that time they should have the benefit of all the sun there is, so as to build up plenty of well-ripened growths.

Where plants are kept permanently in pots, it is a good plan to give an occasional feed of liquid manure during the summer, which will make the leaves of really good appearance, and any repotting necessary can be carried out either in March or September, using a compost made up of sandy loam, some sifted decayed manure or leaf mould and a little bone meal, which will provide nourishment over a long period and just when required.

As something of a change, the foliage can be used for table decoration, for although the flowers of the scented varieties are not particularly large or decorative, the foliage is definitely ornamental.

It is true to say that whether grown in the greenhouse, conservatory or when bedded out, the scented Geranium seems to act as a kind of magnet, for they compel the onlooker, including the most uninterested in plant growing, to touch the foliage and thereby obtain a refreshing perfume. Much has been written and said about the loss of scent in the musk, sweet peas and heliotrope, but such a charge has and never will be made concerning the scented-leaved Geraniums. There is no typical variety, for the habit of growth and shape of foliage is very diverse indeed, and in all cases the scent is "held" by the leaves, which, however, once they are lightly pressed or rubbed, yield their scent, which, of course, is really because the rubbing has forced out the aromatic oils contained in the leaf tissues.

It is often possible to find, particularly in the windows of cottages in the country, really handsome scented-leaved varieties, and there is no doubt that this type of Geranium is as popular to-day as it was during the reign of Charles I, for it was at that time—1632, to be exact—that sailors and travellers first brought this particular type of plant from South Africa to England. It was not, however, until the Victorian period that they came to be grown by the cottager. Until that time, they were possessed mainly by the better-off classes. In the pleasure

Photo: D. F. Merrett

PLATE V. Geranium Wallichianum Buxton's Blue.

PLATE VI. A Collection of Geraniums showing a greatly
differing habit of growth and colour.

PLATE VII. Ideal shoots for cuttings as taken from plants.

PLATE VIII. The cuttings prepared for insertion.

grounds of big houses, where social functions were held, it was the custom to have planted along the garden path, during the summer, a variety of scented-leaved Pelargoniums, so that the leaves could be touched or picked as guests walked through the gardens.

Undoubtedly the most widely grown of the scenteds at the present time is *Pelargonium Capitatum*, which is referred to in the chapter on the uses of the Geranium.

It is much grown in Algeria and parts of France, where an oil or essence is extracted and used in perfume making. This essence is sometimes used in place of the Attar of Roses perfume, since it is less expensive and therefore of economic value in making up many choice perfumes.

P. Capitatum can frequently be seen growing in greenhouses and conservatories, and the plants will, when planted outdoors during the summer months, develop into very big specimens, and produce a plentiful supply of orchid-like flowers, while it is a plant which stands quite a lot of rough treatment.

P. Graveolens is worth mentioning, although it does not seem to be much grown, or at least catalogued, at the present time. It is sometimes referred to as the old-fashioned Rose Geranium, and makes a tallish, compact plant, with well-cut heart-shaped foliage and small purplish white blooms with purple veins. This species has many forms, all of which emit scents which are rose-like. These include *Graveolens Camphorum*, with deeply cut camphory-rose perfume, and Lady Plymouth, a variegated form, the silvery grey leaves having pale yellow margins.

The lemon-scented Geraniums are well known, but here again, there are a number of species in which the habit of growth and depth of perfume varies. *P. Crispum Major*, sometimes known as Prince Rupert, makes a handsome plant of rather columnar growth with single orchid-purple flowers. Variegated Prince Rupert has light green leaves with a narrow border of pale yellow, and *P. Crispum Minor* is the Finger Bowl Geranium, with many small ornamental leaves and pale yellow flowers. *P. Citriodorum*, or Prince of Orange, forms a bushy plant with bright green fan-shaped foliage, the good-sized flowers being white tinged with pale pink.

The rather trailing stems of *P. Nervosum* have dark green lime-scented foliage and lavender flowers with darker shading. *P. tomentosum*, with its highly attractive, large, rather woolly

3

leaves, has a wonderful peppermint scent, while it has a form known as Joy Lucile in which the leaves are triangularly lobed and emit a mint-like scent. *P. Denticulatum* is another species with very finely cut leaves which are ideal for florists' work, the perfume being quite strong but indeterminable.

Coming to the fruit-scented sorts, *P. Fragrans* has small white flowers and sage-green leaves and a nutmeg smell, as also has Lady Mary or *limoneum*. Pretty Polly is almond perfumed; *Scabrum*, apricot; Filbert, nut scented; *Parviflorum*, coconut; *Odoratissimum*, pepper scented. Shottesham Pet smells of filberts, while *P. Torento* has pinkish-lavender flowers with a scent reminding one of ginger.

We can only mention a few of the Pelargoniums with pungent scents, and first comes Clorinda, which is probably the largest flowered of all the scenteds, since the rosy blooms are almost as big as the named bedding Zonals. The leaves emit a distinct eucalyptus-like perfume. Strong growing with dark centred broad leaves, Endsleigh has a sharp, rather peppery smell. *P. Abrotanifolium* smells of southernwood; *P. grossularioides* is gooseberry scented; *P. Rapaceum* and Shrubland Pet remind one of parsley; while there are many forms of *P. Quercifolium*, the well-known Oak-leaved Geranium, so popular as a window-sill plant.

P. Grandula has been described as having both a rose and balsam-like scent. *P. Triste* is the species mentioned on page 8 as having been brought to Britain from South Africa by John Tradescant. Difficult to find nowadays, the plant has finely cut leaves and small green and yellow flowers, and because of its dirty appearance, has been referred to as the Sad Geranium. Although these are by no means all the species and varieties with perfumed leaves, sufficient have been mentioned to show how wide is the range of such plants available.

It is sometimes difficult to fix the scent with some varieties, and where a number of plants are being grown together those with the stronger aroma tend to blot out the more delicate perfume of others.

No special culture is called for, and although they can be propagated from seed, cuttings prepared in the usual way form an easy means of increasing stock. The plants appreciate plenty of sun and light and will grow really well, making bushy specimens, even when kept in quite small pots.

It ought to be remembered that the strength of perfume does

vary according to the temperature, some species emitting more when there is greater heat or at different times of the day. In addition, some leaves need only to be touched to make them give their scent, while others require to be actually bruised. The scented-leaved Geraniums will provide a supply of cut leaves throughout the year, and apart from the use of the leaves as potpourri, a few brought into the house at any time of the year always cause interest and comment, and few persons can resist the temptation to touch or rub them, thus releasing a pleasing perfume.

13

SHOW OR REGAL PELARGONIUMS

BOUND up with the Geranium revival is the greatly increased interest in the Show Pelargoniums, which, correctly speaking, should be referred to as *P. domesticum.*

I have not been able to trace the origin of the name Regal, and can only assume that it was first applied in reference to the stately appearance of this class of Pelargoniums, although it would appear that a number of species have been used in hybridising to bring the Regal or Show Pelargonium to its present state.

These species include *P. Angulosum,* a strong grower which has been known for long over 200 years, *P. Cucullatum* and *P. grandiflorum.* The Show varieties seem always to have been regarded as exclusively greenhouse plants, but they may be, and certainly are, grown outdoors in the flower garden during the summer. When this is done they can be most effective when planted among groups of other subjects; in fact, they give a much more restful appearance than many of the gaudy summer-flowering plants sometimes used, especially as the leaves of some sorts are quite attractive even when the plants are out of flower.

Whilst the plants, indoors, flower to their fullest extent from April to June, if, when planted outdoors, they are given the background of a fence or low wall, they will be encouraged to keep on blooming, and if the flowers are constantly removed when they are past their best, the supply of colour is prolonged by the regular production of fresh heads.

The construction of the petals is quite different from that of the Zonal Geraniums, for they are altogether heavier and closer, and perhaps it was their velvety appearance which made the flowers especially attractive to the Victorians. It ought to be said here that the Show or Regal varieties are not winter flowering, and it would appear to be useless to try and make them so. One of the great drawbacks in cultivating them is their susceptibility to attacks by green and white fly. When growing in a greenhouse in which there is a variety of subjects, it will be found that the pests always go first for these Pelargoniums and occasionally will not touch any other plants. Details of pests, prevention and control, will be found in Chapter 17.

These Regal, Show or Fancy Pelargoniums were at one time separate species, but the uniting of several of these caused the distinctive divisions to be lost in the one group of attractive varieties. Popularly known in the United States as Martha or Lady Washington Geraniums, they take in a wide colour range, and although their flowering period is shorter than that of the Zonals, in many respects, including their shape and beauty, these Show varieties are the loveliest of all Geraniums.

They make really good specimens and in many cases the velvety textured petals form a flower which is three to four inches or more in diameter. There are some varieties of which the flowers are suitable for using in bouquets and other floral make-ups, while, of course, a well-grown pot plant of any good Regal Pelargonium will never fail to prove attractive, especially as in most cases there are several shades of colour in the petals. Since this species is liable to produce rather taller, longer-jointed stems than the Zonals, it is a good plan, unless standard or shaped plants are being grown, to maintain a constant supply of young stems by taking cuttings annually, and thus be able to discard plants which have grown very tall or have become otherwise badly shaped. Personally, I have found that the best way of keeping plants in good condition is to cut them back hard after they have flowered and when the "wood" has ripened.

Occasionally it is as well to root prune, as detailed in the chapter on propagation, while a few applications of liquid manure from the time new growth commences early in the

year, will be well rewarded by stronger growth and bigger
flowers with more brilliant markings.

As to compost and propagation, both are dealt with in the
chapters on these subjects, and there is nothing in the needs of
the plants in these two matters which presents any difficulties
to the keen grower.

This is not the place to give a tremendously long list of
varieties, but the following names and brief description do
give an indication of the sorts available, although it is not in
any way intended to include all the best varieties, although
those mentioned are really dependable in every way.

Black Knight.   Black velvety, pansy-red.
Bridesmaid.   White, with faint darker markings.
Carisbrooke.   Fine rose-pink with wine-coloured markings.
Glorious.   A delightful flesh-pink.
Marylyn.   Having huge flowers of azalea-pink.
Lord Bute or Purple Rose.   Rich purple with picotee edge.
Rhodomine.   Rhododendron mauve and pink.
Sugar Plum.   Attractive shading of blush to strawberry-
pink.
William Pascoe.   Salmon, blotched maroon.
Wootton.   A cherry-crimson of high merit.

It would easily be possible to give details not only of the ten
varieties mentioned above, but of a long list of most desirable
sorts, many with attractive pencillings and blotchings. However, those indicated will prove sufficient to show something of
the range available, and the catalogue of any good specialist
grower will be found to contain upwards of 100 really fine
varieties. It is again stressed that as with the other sections of
Pelargoniums, it is a good plan to take a few cuttings every
year and thus maintain a stock of young, healthy, free-flowering
plants, and be able to discard specimens which are passing their
best, which frequently happens when plants are more than
three or four years old.

Properly grown, it is certain that the Regal or Show Pelargoniums are worth an important place in any selection of
plants for greenhouse decoration, while they are ideal for ex-
hibiting as specimen plants. All varieties flower freely in fresh,
airy houses, but soon begin to deteriorate if kept in a close,
dry atmosphere.

Experiments have proved that with this class of Pelargonium early spring is definitely the best time to take cuttings, which should come from "wood" well ripened in the previous autumn. Although a number of these plants are usually grown, and kept by themselves, when Regal Pelargoniums are used as pot plants for the house, a single plant of any of the good, named varieties, adds a welcome touch of colour when placed among a group of foliage plants.

As with the other sections of Pelargoniums, Regals should be rather underpotted, for it has certainly been proved that they flower much more freely when the roots are pot-bound and are doing their best to come through the sides of the pot! The reason that some sorts are said to be shy bloomers is that they have been given too much root room, and it therefore appears that, other things being right and the compost not being too rich, anything which tends to keep the roots rather restricted or controlled, is likely to lead to increased flowering.

14

UNUSUAL, QUAINT AND RARE GERANIUMS

APART from the many Geraniums which have been dealt with in their respective classes, there are quite a number of really attractive varieties which cannot be placed in any of these sections. This chapter, therefore, deals with such odd and un-classified species and varieties, and it takes in some which are not only of a different habit of growth but those which have quite unconventional flowers.

First there are the Poinsettias, or Cactus-flowered Geraniums, which are characterised by the curled petals on the single or double flowers. There are a number of named varieties taking in the following colours: rose, red, scarlet, white and orange. The first of these were recorded about the year 1900, although none are at all common at the present time. The best varieties include Double Poinsettia, with rolled and twisted red petals. To keep the plants shapely, it is best to regularly shorten the stems to induce plenty of lateral growth. The Pink Poinsettia is particularly free flowering, as is Southern Cross, which has quite large double, curled, pink flowers. One of the strangest growing of all Cactus-flowering sorts is Noel, a really attractive double white.

Some newer varieties of American origin in this section are Mischief, a double orange-scarlet with dark leaves; Puff, a double white, said to be especially good as a pot plant; and Red Spider, scarlet with deep foliage and particularly free flowering.

Another striking section consists of the so-called Bird's Egg varieties, which were also introduced about the year 1900. The flowers of all varieties are freely speckled with red and therefore quite different to the markings on any other variety. Sorts at present available include Double Pink Bird's Egg, of which the flowers are borne in large clusters; Single Pink Bird's Egg is rose with a white centre, all the petals having small rose-red dots; Mrs. J. Knight is single, pale pink and very free flowering, and although a slow grower, makes compact plants.

A group known as the New Life Geraniums have been in cultivation since about 1870. It appears to have commenced with a sport from Vesuvius and had variegated flowers. This first sport was named New Life, and subsequently itself produced other sports, including a double. Vesuvius itself, which is not the same as Black Vesuvius, makes a bushy, compact plant with bright scarlet flowers. Double New Life is curious, with scarlet and white petals on the compact plants, while New Life itself is a single, of which the petals are flecked red and white, or sometimes all are red or all white. None of these varieties is well known at the present time, all are in fact quite scarce.

Having the appearance of a single carnation, and sometimes known as Sweet William, the variety Jeanne bears single, deep salmon-pink flowers, each petal being well serrated. It makes a very lovely plant and its attractive flowers are freely produced. In the same class are Cerise Carnation, of which the double flowers really do resemble a carnation, and Madame Thibaut, producing smallish single flowers reminding one of a single pink. In this old sort, the flowers are white on opening, but pass off through pale to deep pink. Mr. Wren is a unique variety, carrying strong, single, light red flowers, of which the petals have an irregular white border. Whilst it cannot be called very free flowering, it is so unusual that it is well worth growing.

There is a small but very attractive section of Pelargoniums known as the Rose Bud varieties. These are very distinctive, having small double flowers resembling rambler roses on a very small scale. They are particularly valuable as being out of the ordinary and most suitable for cutting, while they are first class for buttonholes, a great point in their favour being that, since they are fully double, the little blooms last considerably longer than the ordinary single Geraniums with their fewer petals which fall more easily.

There are several varieties, including Red Rambler, cerise red, and carried in good-sized clusters, making them look exactly like very tiny rambler roses; Pink Rosebud, pink; Rosebud, purplish crimson; and Scarlet Rosebud, or Supreme by which name it is sometimes known, a fine crimson-scarlet, although still rather expensive.

Somewhat difficult to classify, there are a number of interesting species or varieties which are worthy of mention, if only in some cases because of their unusualness. Among these is *Pelargonium Gibbosum*, frequently referred to as the Gouty Geranium or the Knotty Stork's Bill, on account of its swollen joints or nodes. It has rather brittle leaves and yellowish green flowers, which emit an attractive citron-like perfume in the evening. Somewhat similar is the species *P. Dasycaule*, but the flowers have distinctive maroon markings, while the foliage is rather hairy. *P. Inquinans*, long reputed to be one of the forbears of the modern Zonal Geraniums, is sometimes to be had, although perhaps the single red flowers are not as attractive as many others. *P. Echinatum* is sometimes known as the Cactus-stemmed or Bristly Geranium because of its prickly, stubbly, grey-green stem. It will often flower in the winter and has a habit of developing underground tuberous roots. This species is also known as the Sweetheart Geranium, due to the fact that the upper white petals are marked with a crimson-maroon blotch, which sometimes appears to resemble the shape of a heart.

P. Kewensis, which, as the name indicates, originated from Kew Gardens, where it is usually to be seen planted in plenty, produces single, dark red flowers in abundance and has unusually small leaves, which makes the plant really distinctive.

One of the varieties raised by the late Mr. Langley Smith is *P. Catford Belle*, a miniature grower producing mauve-pink

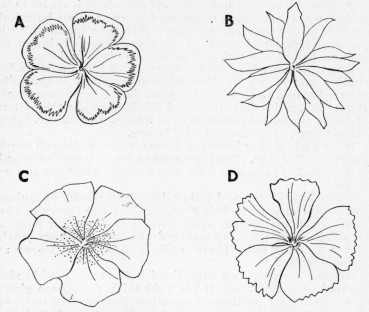

ILLUSTRATING FLOWERS OF UNUSUAL PELARGONIUMS
(A) MR. WREN, (B) POINSETTIA, (C) BIRD'S EGG, (D) JEANNE

flowers, which have a darker mark at the base of each petal. *P. Cotyledonis* is a native of St. Helena, although there are instances of its appearance elsewhere. It is remarkable for its unusually bright and colourful foliage from August onwards, the scarlet and bronze hues making it appear as if the leaves are about to burst into flames. The rather odd-looking greenish yellow flowers appear in good-sized clusters from early June onwards.

P. Tricolor Arboren makes a showy plant with greenish grey leaves and during June and July, smallish flowers of unusual colouring appear. The upper petals are a wine-red colour and the lower one red with black spots in the centre. The plant is of rather drooping habit and therefore first class for trailing over the side of pots or other containers, where the cascade-like growths prove very effective.

P. Schotti is another fine plant and one which is always to be found in the collections maintained by the various botanical gardens of our country. It forms a shrub-like specimen, with greyish leaves, which nicely set off the well-spaced clusters of carmine flowers, of which each petal has a black marking.

There are some Pelargonium species with tuberous roots, including one known as Miss Stapleton's, which is generally believed to be a variety of *Echinatum*, the Cactus-stemmed sort. It has thick, rather juicy stems and dahlia-like roots, the clusters of dainty magenta-mauve flowers, in spite of their colour, being really dainty, attractive and long lasting.

It has a white form known as Album, which is also well worth growing. *P. Triste*, already referred to, has tuberous roots and it is normal to propagate it by root cuttings, which are easy to secure.

Other little-known and rather difficult to classify Geranium species and varieties include *P. Salmonium*, also known as The Boar, which has longish stems, making it appear to be of a climbing habit; the small coral-red blooms have upper petals veined a deeper red. There is also a darker form known as Salmonium Red.

Another variety occasionally listed is *P. Skelley's Pride*, also referred to as *P. Flame*. It has quite thick, dark green glossy leaves and rather small single vermilion flowers. Not really of the appearance that one associates with Geraniums, *P. Tricolor Arborea* is an altogether attractive plant, having greyish green leaves and, being quite different from any other species, with flowers of a shape which is not unlike that of a butterfly. These appear during May and June and as the name indicates take in three shades of colour.

Apart from Black Vesuvius, the fairly well-known variety mentioned elsewhere, there are a number of miniature Zonal Geraniums; these are not just semi-dwarf or compact-growing kinds, but are naturally very small growing, making them entirely different from other types. The mature plants are rarely more than a few inches high. Although fairly well known in the United States, they are not much grown here as yet. Among the named sorts available are Elf, with small, dark, grey-green leaves having a yellow border and irregularly splashed with scarlet, the flowers of which are a bright scarlet. Fairyland, Imp, Little Darling, Pigmy, Pixie, Sprite, Twinkle are all attractive names of other very dwarf sorts, which perhaps are more for the collector than the average grower. Two new semi-dwarf varieties of American origin are Twinkle, which makes small, bushy plants with leaf-green leaves, which are marked a darker green. It seems to be particularly suited to growing in pots and window boxes.

A hybrid between the dwarf Geranium Black Vesuvius and the species *P. Acetosum*, Tweedledee. makes bushy plants which are of medium size with thin, hard stems. As new growth develops in an upright manner, the older stems become arched with their own weight. The rather lobed, dark green foliage is well set off by the light salmon-pink flowers, which are freely produced in clusters. Tweedledum is almost the same as Tweedledee, the difference being that it has dark salmon flowers.

Another interesting American variety is known as Dark Beauty, which is reckoned to be a form of the species *P. Fruteforum*. Rather small growing, the lobed leaves have a dark centre, while the medium-sized flowers are made up of narrow, single orange-salmon flowers, which are freely borne. Sometimes known as One-in-a-Ring, the variety Distinction has smallish pale green leaves which are prettily serrated and ruffled at the edges. The growth is compact and bushy and the flowers are single, cherry-red. This kind is a variety most suitable for the collector.

P. Radula, which will be found mentioned in the chapter on Scented species and varieties, seems to have a past which has become clouded with the passing of time. Even with the meaning of the name itself there seems to be misunderstanding, foɪ some gardening books give *Radula* as referring to a raspberry leaf, which is incorrect, since the word literally means a rasp, file or scraper, and undoubtedly is purposely used in reference to the rough, stiff, skeleton-looking leaves. In fact, *P. Radula* is often referred to as the skeleton-leaved type and on other occasions as the Crow's Foot Geranium. There are several forms of *Radula*, including Dr. Livingstone, with a strong lemon scent, and Blandfordianum, with glossy green leaves and a musk-like perfume.

It is certain that in the past *P. Denticulatum* has often been grown and offered as *P. Radula*, and this has brought about a considerable amount of confusion. *P. Denticulatum* and its several forms, including the one known as Pheasant's Foot, all have finely cut leaves, although the scent is pine or sometimes rose-like rather than lemon or balsam, while the flowers are lavender with darker markings.

An unusual Pelargonium which can be seen growing at the R.H.S. Wisley gardens is *P. Ardens*, with umbels of small, deep red flowers and rather hairy leaves, and this is yet another example of the fact that there are many interesting Pelargoniums which are all too rarely seen or even known nowadays.

With so many difficult-to-classify species and varieties, which are not hardy and need greenhouse culture, it will possibly be some time before the matter is really clarified. With the increased interest in Geranium culture it is possible that there are a number of species and odd varieties, now unrecognised and little valued, in out of the way country places which will be brought to light again. Anyone who has an unusual Geranium of any kind, would be doing a real service to all Geranium lovers by letting some specialist see their plant.

15

THE ONLY HARDY PELARGONIUM

A PLANT which is rarely, if ever, seen outside botanical gardens is *Pelargonium Endlicherianum*, which I believe to be the only hardy species in existence. It is a native of the limestone alps of the Cilician Taurus and will actually live a long time in quite exposed positions.

Perhaps it is the name itself which is one of the reasons why the plant is not better known or more frequently grown, for it is certain that if it were, it would be much more widely cultivated, since it is not only hardy but beautiful. Undoubtedly, although it is now so rare, means would be found if the demand was sufficient to enable nurserymen to grow and offer this species. The plants like well-drained, fairly rich soil in which there is a good lime content, and the more sun the better.

The plants develop into leafy bushes, of which the rather soft but typically Geranium-like leaves are well scalloped and strongly aromatic. The continuously produced flower stems, from twelve to eighteen inches high, carry clusters of from three

Geranium Lucidum

to six clear carmine-pink flowers, which look well both when grown in the border or in the rock graden. The formation of the blooms always commands a second look on account of the upper petals being so much larger than the lower ones.

The foliage of this plant, which actually received an Award of Merit as long ago as 1901, usually develops attractive autumn colourings, and this is another reason why it deserves greater attention.

16

THE TRUE GERANIUM

REFERENCE has been made to the little Herb Robert, *Geranium Robertianum*, which flourishes at the hedge bases or other shady roadside places. In addition, there is another attractive little species which can frequently be found in hilly limestone districts, where it climbs walls with ease and makes a brave show for several months of the spring and summer. This cheerful little Crane's Bill, is the biennial G. *Lucidum*, with small bright rose-coloured flowers, which appear with great freedom along the six to ten inch sprawling plant stems.

Another small-flowered species, which makes neat little hummocks of growth, is G. *Celticum*; at least, it has long been known under that name, although botanists now say that it is an albino form of G. *Robertianum*. Amid the fern-like foliage there are produced throughout the summer, numerous dainty white flowers on three to four inch stems. Since the plant thrives in a shady, moist position the little white flowers show up well.

Intriguing as these dainty wildings are, it is the larger-growing hardy Crane's Bills which are of the most value in the rock garden or front of the border, as well as in the wild garden.

The best of these I will now mention alphabetically and therefore not necessarily in order of merit. Although all are normally obtainable without difficulty none are troublesome to grow, and the majority will thrive in any good soil and full sun, although most will grow in semi-shade as well. G. *Anemonifolium*, which prefers a sunny, sheltered position, is perhaps the one which should be given a little more care in cultivation. Introduced from Madeira towards the end of the eighteenth century, it will thrive where there is very little soil, especially if given the protection of a wall. It forms large rosettes of showy leaves which colour up well, while from the tall, branching stems there appears very many crimson flowers. G. *Argenteum* has been grown here for more than 250 years. It has attractively cut leaves which are evergreen and these, as the name suggests, are of a silvery colouring. The six inch branching stems produce, just above the foliage, rich pink, saucer-shaped flowers, and there are forms known as Lissadell variety, pu-

pureum and allunagh, which may all be synonymous, showing blooms which are a near crimson colour. The white form is less attractive, since it does not show up its blooms in such contrast to the foliage as do the pinks and crimsons.

G. Armenum is strikingly handsome. Originating in Armenia, it will grow as much as three feet high when given a rich site. The freely produced large flowers, are of a real magenta shade, which is unusual in flowers, the dark centre making the petal colour even more attractive. Not easy to interplant with other more bright colours, such as pinks and reds, *G. Armenum* is most effective when given a niche of its own, where it can flower freely without becoming an eyesore against other plants. It is not invasive and does not require staking.

G. Atlanticum, although little known, is quite pretty, its purple-coloured flowers appearing on twelve to eighteen inch stems surrounded by well-cut, anemone-like leaves.

Altogether smaller growing, *G. Cinerecum*, from the Pyrenees, is somewhat similar to *Armenum* excepting size. Easy to grow, it has greyish green cut leaves and rosy purple flowers on six inch stems. It has a form, which is a native of the Balkans, which is sometimes said to be the finest of the rock garden Geraniums. This is *G. C. Subcaulescens*, with well-formed, clear carmine-coloured flowers, which appear in succession from May until the end of the summer. It does not mind being cut back after flowering; in fact, where this is done, it soon makes plenty of new flower stems. Provided with a well-drained soil and an open sunny position, this species will give of its very best.

G. Dalmaticum is comparatively new to this country and its name will suggest its origin. Its worth was recognised almost as soon as it reached British gardens, since it received a R.H.S. Award of Merit in 1940. Dwarf growing, it is ideal for the rock garden, forming low, shapely mats of well-cut, glossy leaves, which take on pleasing autumn tints. The well-proportioned clear pink flowers are carried on stems of six to eight inches, the prominent dark stamens and stigma adding to the beauty of the blooms. Easy to grow in fairly light soil in the open or on a wall, it is also admirable for growing in a pot or pan, while it is most suitable for the alpine house.

Of *G. Endressii* one must write with caution, for although it is undoubtedly a most desirable species and one which continues to bloom from June until well into the autumn, it does grow very quickly, and if not watched and kept under control it is liable to smother other choicer, smaller-growing subjects.

However, this is a most desirable species for which room should be made, for it carries its lovely bright pink flowers in great abundance. It is best kept off the rockery and given a space at the front of a good wide border, and it always looks well in the wild garden or near the edge of the woodland. There are several good forms of G. *Endressii*, among the best of which are A. T. Johnson, having silvery pink flowers on fifteen inch stems and doing well in both shade and sun; Rose Clair, with salmony rose flowers and of similar habit and Wargrave variety, which produces an abundance of clear pink blooms.

Best suited for growing in the wild garden is G. *Eriostemon* from Russia. This has purple-coloured flowers on twelve to eighteen inch stems. A first-class species, introduced by Reginald Farrer about 1917, has become widely known as G. *Napuligerum*, although it is also frequently catalogued and referred to as G. *Farreri*, which is certainly easier to pronounce and remember. A lovely dwarf alpine, it thrives in a sunny position, where early in the spring it puts out a cluster of dark green, deeply cut leaves. These are quickly followed by branching stems three to four inches high, which bear several large cup-shaped, apple-blossom pink flowers, set off by a cluster of dark anthers. Given a gritty soil in a sunny position G. *Farreri* rarely, if ever, fails to do well.

Flowering from early summer to late autumn is G. *Grandiflorum Alpinum*, sometimes known as Gravetye variety. This again is a rather spreading sort, and should therefore be given ample space to develop. It is, however, so lovely that it is worth any trouble needed in restricting its growth. It likes sun and almost any type of soil, and from early June until late September shows its large, clear blue flowers on stems of twelve inches or more.

Ideal for the wild garden, G. *Ibericum* continuously produces its rich violet-purple flowers on stems eighteen to twenty-four inches high. G. *Kotschyi*, from Armenia, throws up many anemone-like leaves, which, however, contrary to the majority of most species, die down in the autumn. This sort, too, has thick, almost tuber-like roots, and throughout the early summer pushes up its nine inch branching stems of really large lavender-purple flowers, of which the petals are veined with deeper markings.

G. Macrorrhizum, from the Balkans, has a pleasing habit of growth, forming low hummocks of rounded, light green, scented leaves, which usually colour up to a shade of deep red and crimson in the winter. During the early summer the nine inch stems appear, bearing many wide open, clear pink flowers. I have only recently grown the form known as Ingwersen's variety, which is taller, with even larger rosy pink flowers. It is, I think, the best form, although there are others, including *Grandiflorum*, deep pink, and *Album*, having large, pure white flowers with leaves which have a clean, sweet aroma.

G. Phæum is the "Mourning Widow" Geranium of Victorian times. It was so named because of its dark brown flowers, of which each petal has a white spot at the base. This species and its rarer white form, *Album*, grow approximately fifteen to eighteen inches high and both are of most easy culture.

The blue Meadow Crane's Bill, *G. Pratense*, although a wildling, has nevertheless a beautiful flower. Rather rampant in growth, unless kept under control, it looks well when planted in the front of the herbaceous border, where the large, bowl-shaped flowers of clear blue, with a white eye, show up to great advantage. There are now several cultivated forms, which include Mrs. Kendal Clark, pale opal; Silver Queen, silvery blue on vigorous stems thirty inches or more high; and *Album*, with large milk-white flowers on two feet stems. In spite of its name, *G. Pylzowianum*, from China, is pretty. It has one inch wide clear pink flowers on stems of about four or five inches. It is a deciduous species which forms a network of thread-like roots, which although they tend to roam, are so frail as not to cause trouble.

G. Renardii, from the Caucasus Mountains, forms tufts of deeply lobed, grey-green thick leaves. Produced on six to nine inch stems, the charming lavender flowers appear throughout the summer and autumn.

Long known as the Bloody Crane's Bill, *G. Sanguineum* is a rather creeping species with crimson-magenta flowers. It is, however, the form known as *lancastriense*, without which no rock garden is complete. Originally found on the Isle of Walney in Lancashire, the plants bear a very long succession of salmon-pink, cup-shaped flowers set among the dark green leaves. Seen growing alongside some grey foliaged plants it is strikingly effective.

G. Sessiliflorum nigricans, a flat-growing species, is of very easy culture. It has very dark foliage, made more prominent during the summer when the small white flowers develop. G. *Striatum*, of decumbent habit, produces, from May to October, pretty pink flowers with dark veins.

G. *Sylvaticum* is another native, found mostly in the north of England, with purple-blue flowers having crimson veins and appearing on two feet stems during June and July. It is, however, the newer forms of this species which are most worth while. These are *Album*, eighteen inches, the pure white flowers, often having buds which are prettily tinted pale pink, and *roseum*, an unusual clear rose-pink.

G. *Stapfianum* is a handsome little plant, with glossy green leaves which colour up in the autumn, and rosy pink flowers on four inch stems. The form *roseum* is similar, but the blooms are of a crimson-purple colour.

Another larger-growing Geranium is *Viscosissimum*. It looks well towards the front of the herbaceous border, where it can have partial shade and where it produces its two inch wide purple-red flowers on strong stems up to two feet in height.

G. *Wallichianum* was introduced to Britain from Nepal in 1819, and in comparison with some of the other species is not very exciting. The flower stems are inclined to flop or sprawl about, while the blooms themselves, although large, are of an unattractive purple shade. It is, however, the form of *Wallichianum* known as Buxton's variety which should be in every garden. Discovered by the late Mr. Charles Buxton in his garden in Wales, and of course named after him, it became popular as soon as distributed. In fact, it received from the R.H.S. an Award of Garden Merit as long ago as 1925. It can be said to have superseded *Wallichianum* itself, and no wonder, for it produces cup-shaped flowers of a light, yet rich blue, with a showy pure white central ring. It likes a cool but sunny place, and will grow in almost any soil provided it is well drained. It can easily be kept within bounds and freely produces its blooms from June until late autumn. Fortunately it comes true from seed, which is a great point in its favour, seeing that so many others do not do so.

Other quite good but little-known hardy Geraniums include G. *Pyrenaicum*, the Mountain Crane's Bill, with well-divided hairy leaves and reddish mauve flowers; G. *Versicolor*, the pencilled Geranium, having pale pink flowers well veined with red; and G. *Nodosum*, very similar to the previous variety but

with red flowers and smooth stems. Apart from G. *Robertianum,*
already mentioned, there are several other good biennial sorts
often found growing in rough places. Among these are G.
Molle, the Dove's Foot Crane's Bill, usually regarded as a weed;
Columbianum, with straggly growth and rose-pink flowers; and
G. *Dissectum,* the jagged-leaved Crane's Bill, with much
branched stems and divided foliage.

Some of the hardy Geraniums are most useful for planting
beneath and around shrubs to avoid that bare soil appearance,
and there they also help to keep down weeds. In addition,
these plants assist in retaining moisture in the soil, an important point with some subjects which quickly show signs of
any dryness at their roots. Apart from these considerations,
the foliage of certain hardy Geraniums is not only ornamental,
but colours up well in the autumn, and it does seem as though
they like being associated in this way with various shrubs.
Furthermore, these hardy Geraniums do not require frequent
lifting or dividing, neither do they object to a certain amount
of shade or mind being somewhat overhung by the boughs and
branches of the shrubs; in fact, the majority of them are long-
lived and carefree.

Obviously care must be taken to ensure that the flowers of
the species used do not clash with those of the shrubs, although
such combinations can be, and I think are, best selected so that
the flowering times are different, which does away with the
objection sometimes raised that shrubs and trees, which take
up a good deal of room in a small garden, are in colour for so
short a time.

Some of the double forms are reminiscent of the flowers of
long ago, as depicted on old manuscripts and prints, and they
do seem to have an appeal as most appropriate companions for
growing under and around the real old-fashioned types of
shrub roses, as well as some of the attractively coloured rose
species.

Species of hardy Geraniums specially adapted to associating
with shrubs include *Endressii, Grandiflorum, Ibericum, Pratense, Sanguineum* and its forms. These all flower over a long
period, requiring practically no attention when established,
and do not altogether object if their foliage is cut back should
it become too luxuriant or exceed the space allotted to the
plants.

Worthy of mention, too, are two little-known and not frequently found North American hardy species. The first is *G. Erianthum*, which is a native of coastal districts of British Columbia, where it produces from mid-summer onwards pale lavender flowers, the petals being pencil marked a bright reddish violet. Easy to grow in the sheltered rock and scree garden, it is also a delightful plant for the alpine house.

G. Incisum is stronger growing, and makes a good plant for the front of the border. Attaining a height of twelve to eighteen inches, the stems carry really large, deep rose-pink flowers finely pencil-marked with crimson; both stems and leaves being quite hirsute. It is possible to find a number of colour variations from self-sown seedlings, some of which are not of a particularly desirable shade of colour. To maintain a true stock it is essential to propagate by division, although this is not too easy because of the particular shape of the roots.

17

THE HERON'S BILL

ALTHOUGH *Erodium Cicutaricum* is often overlooked or intentionally ignored because it is one of our annual native wild flowers, it nevertheless produces the most charming and graceful little blossoms. Whether one considers the attractive and ornamental foliage, the colour and form of the blooms, or the quaint, rigid, beak-like seed pods, all are equally desirable. It is normally to be found growing either on waste ground, where it seems able to resist drought, or quite frequently among cultivated field crops, where it flowers throughout the summer.

Of semi-upright habit, the stems themselves are usually nine to twelve inches long, although the tops may be only six or seven inches from the ground, owing to their habit of growth. The pink flowers are divided into five, each part having a sepal, petal, stigma and two stamens, one of which is sterile and rudimentary. Both the pinnate leaves and stems are hairy.

The derivation of the word *Cicutaricum* is of much interest, since it comes from *Cicula*, a classical but not the scientific name for hemlock, and was given from the supposed likeness between the leaves of the two plants. *Cicula* is said to have

Erodium Cicutaricum

been so named by Theophrastus and indicates in the Greek, a top or cone, supposedly referring to the connection between the whirling motion of a top and the giddiness which came upon anyone who was foolish enough to allow themselves to taste the poisonous hemlock.

There are many other species, and *E. Moschatum* or the Musky Heron's Bill is considerably larger growing, the flowers being bluish purple, while the well-divided leaves emit a musk-like scent, which of course is indicated by the name.

E. Maritinum is the Sea Heron's Bill, sometimes found growing near the seashore. It is, however, a very small-growing plant, with purple flowers and hairy stems and foliage. In some respects the cultivated Erodiums may be said to be first-class examples of the Geranium family, although some of them shed their petals so quickly that the plants must be frequently looked at to ensure the blooms are not missed. In all cases the Erodium flowers are followed by really large Heron's Bill seed pods, which, when ripe, have a habit of contracting in such a way so as to form a spire, rather as a ripe sweet pea pod behaves. As the pointed seeds, which have stiff hairs all sloping one way, are ejected, when the pods split and twist, they shoot upwards and forwards like an arrow, and as they fall, easily penetrate into the soil, where they germinate.

Contrary to the Pelargoniums, they are quite rare in South Africa, being chiefly natives of North Africa and Europe. Practically all species emit some kind of smell when the foliage is bruised, in some cases being not altogether pleasant. The Erodiums make first-class plants for the rock garden, and are specially valuable in that when established, they have the ability to thrive in a dry or sandy soil where many other subjects will not do well. They look well growing in the crevices of a sunny wall and have the capacity of producing blooms throughout the summer months. There are many species, some of which are very similar and others which are hard to come by. Taking some of the best alphabetically, *E. Chamædrioides roseum* produces throughout the summer a regular show of deep pink flowers, well set among glossy green leaves. *E. Chrysanthum* is undoubtedly one of the loveliest, making little clumps of ferny, silvery green foliage, from which arises attractive little sprays of yellow flowers. *E. Corsicum* is a little taller, the freely borne, small pink flowers coming on four inch stems surrounded by clusters of grey foliage. *E. Hymenodes* has flushed pink petals, of which the upper ones have a reddish brown spot at the base. Growing ten to twelve inches high, the flowers appear from June until the early frosts come. This species is sometimes referred to as *E. Trilobatum.*

E. Manescavii is a native of the Pyrenees and may be regarded as one of the very best. Growing quite large, and there are one or two forms which will develop to eighteen inches or more in diameter, the fern-like leaves provide an excellent foil for the purplish red, almost magenta, blooms which go on from May until September. If carefully placed where the flowers are not likely to clash with the colour of other subjects, they are quite effective. *E. Pelargoniflorum,* growing about one foot high, is not unlike *Hymenodes,* excepting perhaps that the petals have light purplish spots on them, while the sepals have a little tail coming from their points, which is not the case with the latter species. Both seed themselves freely, so that it is really best to keep up a supply of young plants rather than attempt to retain the older plants, which so often are either killed or damaged during the winter. *E. Romanum* commences to flower in the spring and often goes on showing colour until late autumn. Known in this country for well over 200 years, the purplish flowers appear on six to nine inch stems.

18

SOME PELARGONIUM DISEASES

WHILE with some flowers increase in cultivation, new development and improvements have also brought fresh troubles in the way of disease, this is certainly not so with the Pelargonium, which remains of the same good constitution and continues to be just as resistant to disease as it ever was.

Without wishing to give too much prominence to diseases, for fear of conveying the impression that Pelargoniums are troublesome to keep healthy, it is nevertheless necessary to mention diseases which may possibly appear, although it must not be taken for granted that they are bound to occur. In fact, many Geranium growers have cultivated the plant for years without any trace of trouble.

Even so, it is well to know what are the possibilities in this connection, for early identification enables any complaint to be dealt with immediately and therefore prevents it spreading. It should be the aim of the grower, whether he cultivates six or a hundred plants, to begin with a clean healthy stock, for then there will be less likelihood of the plants contracting any disease and the greater will be the possibility of recovery should any plants be attacked.

Sometimes a plant will flag and become discoloured for no apparent reason, and in such cases, provided it is not due to dryness or pests attacking the roots, the best plan is to destroy it.

Good growing conditions should always be provided, with the plants being allowed plenty of room and light, and given good ventilation at all times. Use common sense in watering, so that the soil does not become either sour and waterlogged or dry and hard. Avoid feeding with forcing artificial fertilisers and make sure that all decaying leaves are removed.

There are very few gardeners who have not had some experience of the disease commonly known as blackleg, which is sometimes referred to as grey mould. This is of fungus origin and there are many types, and the one which attacks Pelargoniums will also affect lettuces, marrows, melons and tomatoes, and is scientifically known as *Botrytis Cinerea*. Quite often the spores of this fungus gain a hold on the lower stems as a result of damage or even the bruising of the outer tissues, and since the spores are very persistent and can remain active for a long time, it is important to be scrupulously clean at all times, keeping all decayed leaves and rubbish cleared away from the plants and avoiding a close, damp atmosphere. Since dampness seems to be essential for the active life of the fungi, precautions must be taken to avoid careless watering. Few of us can appreciate how tiny are the spores or how rapidly they increase, or, again, how very quickly they are to settle and develop on a congenial host. This, of course, is an additional reason why cleanliness and conditions which encourage sturdy, firm growth are essential.

Since the spores are often water-borne, care must be taken in watering both newly inserted cuttings and established plants, for if moisture cannot get away from the surface there is a greater chance that trouble will commence. This, incidentally, is another reason why the compost used should be fairly open and contain plenty of silver sand so as to allow the moisture to pass through fairly easily. Possibility of blackleg also makes it important to prepare cuttings with great care, for the disease will often enter at the base if it is left ragged and not severed immediately beneath a joint. Once the rooting system is developing well, there is less likelihood of the disease gaining hold, and although it will sometimes appear on shoots which have been cut or stopped, well-grown plants kept under good conditions are rarely affected.

Since there are various forms of this fungus disease there are also differing evidences of the infection, for although the most usual indication of the presence of the disease is the blackening and rapid decay of the plant stem at soil level and of the leaves, it is sometimes first seen as a spot discoloration of the foliage, which are more likely to appear when the plants are crowded together and when they remain cold and damp. *Botrytis* will frequently enter the scar where leaves have been removed and even at the point where stopping has been done, and in fact at any place where the plants have become soft, decayed or weakly. Plants out of condition due to unbalanced feeding, bad light and overwatering, also become an easy prey to *Botrytis*. Infection and spread of the disease almost always develop under glass, although it can be carried out of doors by the plants.

It is probable the disease known as leafy gall, which not only attacks Pelargoniums but chrysanthemums and other plants, is caused by one of the same parasitic fungus as that which brings about blackleg or *Botrytis* disease, although the scientific name of the bacteria or fungus which is the cause of this particular disease is *Corynebacterium fascians*. This will sometimes result in much fasciation or the fusing together of two or more stems, or will cause the plant to remain stunted or, typically, it will induce development of a leafy gall, which is found growing at soil level beside the stem. It may be that some kind of growth hormone is produced in the plant, the reaction of which, is to stop normal growth, while it may also be that the food being carried in the sap is used by the disease spores.

Although leafy gall is, up to the present, regarded as incurable, experiments are being carried out which show promise of being effective. In the meantime, no cuttings should be taken from plants showing the least symptoms of the disease; in fact, the safest plan is to burn them with the soil in which they are growing, thus minimising the possibility of spreading the trouble.

Where any fungus disease is suspected or there are the slightest signs of its appearance, steps should be taken to arrest its development at once, although all plants on which the disease has really got a hold ought to be destroyed without delay. Fortunately there is a preparation known as Folosan, a non-poisonous dust fungicide, manufactured by Messrs. Bayer Agriculture, Ltd., which is invaluable in checking *Botrytis*. It is perfectly safe to use and has no harmful effects on the most tender of plants. Folosan arrests the growth of the fungus or mildew, stops the production of spores from an existing infection and, a most important point, prevents the germination of the "sclerotia", those hard, black disease specks which can remain dormant in the soil for a very long while and then reappear to do their harmful work.

In using the powder the aim should be to cover the surface
of all the foliage, which can normally be done by using a
bellows or rotary type duster. Having blown the powder into
the air, keep the greenhouse closed for about half an hour to
allow the Folosan to settle. A normal rate of application is
up to a quarter of an ounce per square yard of floor area, each
application of the powder being effective for ten to fourteen
days.

Occasionally on some plants, the stem becomes greatly en-
larged and distorted, and they in turn produce distorted flower
trusses. This trouble is sometimes referred to as *Elephantiasis*;
quite an appropriate name. As yet little seems to be known as
to the origin or prevention of the trouble, which frequently
only affects one part of the plant. It may have some relation
to the intake of moisture or chemicals by the roots, and the
plants not being able to make full and normal use of them, the
result being a swelling of the cells. Obviously it would be
unwise to take cuttings from any plant showing the slightest
signs of *Elephantiasis*; in fact, here again the best policy is to
burn such plants

Of recent years there has been much said and written about
virus diseases of plants. Certainly these seem to be on the
increase and they have caused considerable concern to dahlia,
chrysanthemum and tomato growers. So far, little is known of
virus trouble in Pelargoniums, although they certainly can be
affected, and in bedding varieties, the disease often shows itself
by a mottling of the leaves and stunted growth; but from personal experience it does not seem to be a trouble which spreads
rapidly, for plants which have shown unmistakable signs of
virus disease, do not appear to have given it to other nearby
specimens. In fact, the symptoms have often entirely dis-
appeared, although it may very well be that in such cases the
disease is still actually present in the plants and would reappear if growing conditions are other than really good.

The spread of virus is often caused by the use of an infected
knife or other tools, but greenfly are undoubtedly greatly instrumental in increasing the trouble and should always be destroyed before they have time to increase.

There is one virus disease which is commonly known as
Pelargonium leaf curl, which produces pale yellowish spots
which later become larger and darker in colour. Frequently,
these spots turn to dark brown when the leaf tissues die. The

markings are accompanied by the leaf puckering badly and almost curling, which makes it easy to identify affected plants. Often such plants will make new growth, which appears perfectly healthy, but of course the disease is still present, and should cuttings be taken from such plants, the following season they will exhibit the symptoms of the virus disease.

Both the Ivy-leaved varieties and the larger-flowered Regals seem to possess a considerable resistance to viruses. Here, again, aphis, which are so frequently found on glasshouse crops, are believed to be the vector. It is impossible to take too much care in seeking to prevent or keep down virus troubles, and it is certainly a good plan to sterilise knives or other tools used in taking cuttings. All plants showing signs of any of the mentioned leaf symptoms should be immediately burned. Zonal Geraniums can also be affected by cucumber mosaic, a virus trouble more prevalent than is often supposed.

It is never wise to grow cucumbers and Geraniums in the same greenhouse unless it is possible to start with absolutely clean stocks, and regular measures must be taken to keep down aphis of all kinds. Undoubtedly the old-time gardeners who used to talk about cucumbers giving Geraniums "the yellows" were wiser than they knew, or perhaps they had more knowledge than is often credited to them!

19

PESTS AND THEIR DESTRUCTION

IT is sometimes said, that in writing about any particular plants it is unwise to refer in detail to any pests, which may possibly be troublesome, for fear of giving the prospective grower the impression that he is up against a long and difficult battle in seeking to cultivate the flower of his choice.

I certainly do not support this theory, for if we have a liking for any particular plant we shall continue to want to grow it, although recognising that possible difficulties may arise. In fact, to be able to cultivate successfully plants which are not too easy, is an ideal which all real gardeners desire to achieve.

Besides this, any book on a particular subject should, I think, deal with all aspects of culture and any possible difficulties or problems should not be ignored. Therefore, even in this simple handbook, a short chapter on pests and their destruction, is deemed not only desirable but essential.

Because of this, it must not be assumed that the Geranium is especially prone to insect attacks. In fact, grown under good, clean, healthy conditions it is really surprising how free from pests the plants are, and even in these days when fresh pests seem to be appearing on many widely grown garden plants, the Geranium has remained almost untouched.

There are circumstances when it is necessary to identify and deal with the few pests which occasionally do appear, and it is the purpose of this chapter, which is intentionally written in simple, non-technical terms, to enable the reader to easily put into operation the measures suggested for their identification, control and prevention and so maintain a stock of healthy plants of pleasing appearance.

As it is to many other plants, greenfly is enemy number one, and they seem to appear from nowhere. They increase at a phenomenal rate, and if left undisturbed will work very quickly indeed. These pests usually first settle on the undersides of the leaves or in the tender growing point, making the foliage curled and distorted, and by sucking, as they do, the sap from the leaves, bring about reddish markings and spots and occasionally damage the flower buds too. Apart from all this, they freely act as agents in carrying the virus of mosaic disease and are probably the carriers of other troubles too, so that even from this aspect alone, it is essential to prevent the possible increase and spread of greenfly. As a rule the Zonals are not often attacked, but the flies will certainly go for the Regals, and what I think is most surprising, where there is a choice, will often settle on the Scented-leaved sorts in preference to any other, which rather contradicts the general belief that plants with perfumed foliage, act as a deterrent to pests.

The range of present-day greenfly killers is extremely large and it becomes almost puzzling for the average gardener to know what to select. Generally speaking, I am not in favour of the modern practice of using poisonous sprays on every possible occasion, for it is undoubtedly true that besides destroying the pests aimed at, many insecticides kill the predators which have been created to keep down many harmful insects, and thus a vicious circle is formed, whereby it becomes necessary to continually spray and dust because the natural balance of predators and pests has been broken. There have been a number of instances reported in the national press where the continued use of D.D.T. and other insecticides has led to the destruction of bees and other useful insects.

What can one use on Geraniums? Nicotine is certainly good if applied in moderation, and the brand known as Mortopal is a really first-class greenfly killer if used strictly in accordance with directions on the tin. The old-fashioned quassia extract and soft soap is good and safe, as is Sybol. The best method, particularly if using Mortopal or any other insecticide wash, is to spray in the evening, being most careful to reach the undersides of the leaves and centres of the plants. Then cleanse the plants by spraying with clear water the following morning, thus avoiding the possibility of the flower or foliage becoming discoloured.

Do this as soon as the first aphis is seen and thus make eradication much easier. Make sure to spray any other plants in the same house and also into any holes and crevices there may be in the greenhouse woodwork and walls. The fumigation of the greenhouse with nicotine or other shreds is also effective, but here again it is essential to follow the manufacturer's instructions.

Whitefly will, on occasion, concentrate on the Regal varieties, but rarely on the Zonals. It is, of course, easy to detect when they are flying about or settling on the foliage, and this is another instance where speed is necessary in dealing with the pests, for they also increase very rapidly. Fumigation is a means of control, and there are a number of special whitefly killers, which, however, if wrongly used, may damage both flowers and foliage as well as other plants, so that again, the maker's instructions must be followed in detail.

Sometimes caterpillars will eat the foliage of Geraniums, and once damage is noticed, regular examination of the leaves is advisable, so as to be able to destroy the eggs, which, if left, will soon hatch out to bring another generation of caterpillars into being. Where convenient, shake the plants over newspaper so as to dislodge any of the pests. They can then easily be destroyed, while the now rarely practised job of examining the plants at night under artificial light, will prove most rewarding in revealing the caterpillars. Any of the good insecticides forcibly sprayed on to the plants will usually prove effective in destroying the caterpillars.

Very occasionally mealy bug and thrips will appear, but since they usually only do so as a result of neglect and the accumulation of dirt, they are not likely to trouble the enthusiastic Geranium grower, who will, as his normal routine, ensure that clean conditions and a buoyant atmosphere are provided for his treasures. With the former, fumigating with nicotine or the use of derris are usually effective, while with thrips the use of D.D.T. emulsion or smoke "bombs" will normally stamp out the pests, which are more likely to appear in a hot, dry atmosphere.

Although red spider is not uncommon in greenhouses and conservatories, this is another pest which only thrives under close, dry conditions, and since Geraniums really prefer a rather moist atmosphere there is rarely any trouble from this pest. Should it be suspected, extra moisture applied, not only as needed by the plants, but also to the pots and staging, will do much to prevent the Geraniums being harmed. The spraying of the plants with pyrethrum powder, if applied to both sides of the leaves, usually proves to be quite effective in destroying red spider, especially if, as already suggested, dry conditions are avoided.

Woodlice will also sometimes damage Geraniums, and since they are to be found almost everywhere, both indoors and out, regular steps should be taken to keep them in check. All decaying wood and rubbish should be removed and any other likely hiding-place cleared away. The old-fashioned method of applying paraffin to the place where the woodlice are known to be frequent, will prove most helpful.

On very infrequent occasions blackfly will settle on greenhouse Geraniums, and these may be eradicated by the same means as recommended for whitefly.

INDEX